Economic Interdependence and Conflict in World Politics

Innovations in the Study of World Politics

Series Editor
Zeev Maoz, University of California, Davis

Advisory Board
Michael Barnett, University of Wisconsin, Madison
Deborah Larson, UCLA
Brett Ashley Leeds, Rice University
Jack Levy, Rutgers University

This series provides a forum for the publication of original theoretical, empirical, and conceptual studies that seek to chart new frontiers in the field of international relations. The key emphasis is on innovation and change. Books in the series will offer insights on and approaches to a broad range of issues facing the modern world, in an effort to revolution-ize how contemporary world politics are studied, taught, and practiced.

Economic Interdependence and Conflict in World Politics

Mark J. C. Crescenzi

LEXINGTON BOOKS

A Division of
ROWMAN & LITTLEFIELD PUBLISHERS, INC.
Lanham • Boulder • New York • Toronto • Oxford

LEXINGTON BOOKS

A division of Rowman & Littlefield Publishers, Inc.
A wholly owned subsidiary of The Rowman & Littlefield Publishing Group, Inc.
4501 Forbes Boulevard, Suite 200
Lanham, MD 20706

PO Box 317
Oxford
OX2 9RU, UK

Copyright © 2005 by Lexington Books

British Library Cataloguing in Publication Information Available

Library of Congress Cataloging-in-Publication Data

Crescenzi, Mark J. C., 1970-
  Economic interdependence and conflict in world politics / Mark J.C. Crescenzi.
    p. cm.—(Innovations in the study of world politics)
  Includes bibliographical references and index.
  ISBN 0-7391-1038-1 (cloth : alk. paper)—ISBN 0-7391-1039-X (pbk. : alk. paper)
  1. International economic relations. 2. International trade. 3. International relations. 4.
Conflict management. 5. Military policy. I. Title. II. Series.
HF1379.C755 2005
337—dc22   2005016165

Printed in the United States of America

For Anita, and my parents. Their support made this book possible.

Acknowledgments

I would like to thank Dina Zinnes and Robert Muncaster for mentoring me patiently and for providing such an incredible research environment for learning. And thanks to Paul Diehl and William Berhnard for their guidance, patience, and encouragement. Thanks also to Anita Crescenzi and Andrew Enterline for their unwavering support. This research would have never made it to Lexington Books without the help of Zeev Maoz. The research in this book takes advantage of publicly available data, and for that I would like to thank all the generous scholars who make their data available for the sake of furthering knowledge. Finally, the Merriam Laboratory for Analytic Political Research at the University of Illinois, Urbana-Champaign kindly provided resources that had a fundamental impact on the research in this book.

Contents

Tables

Figures

1
Introduction:
A Persistent Puzzle

> The processes that take place in a system are affected by its structure. . . . The preferences of the states predispose them toward certain strategies; the structure of the system provides opportunities and constraints. (Robert Keohane and Joseph Nye, 1989: 261)

> Here, as in other matters, there is safety in numbers. (Kenneth Waltz, 1979: 147)

Economic Interdependence:
Recipe for Peace or Source of Conflict?

The world is experiencing a growth of economic exchange between nations that has its roots in the end of World War II. According to *The Economist* (1997), global trade volume has increased sixteen-fold in less than fifty years, almost three times the increase in total output. Regional integration, such as the European Union (EU), the Asian Pacific Economic Cooperation (APEC), and the North American Free Trade Act (NAFTA), is fueling pockets of economic activity for the sake of greater prosperity and competition. At a recent gathering of APEC members in Auckland, New Zealand, the member states pledged to continue their efforts to open up markets for exchange and develop their economic ties (APEC, 1999). Their motivation is both simple and powerful: to increase wealth through economic exchange. The gains from trading goods and services are a clear result of the comparative advantage of nations. Open economic exchange increases the efficient allocation of resources for production, and increases the world's ability to produce goods and services, thus increasing the goods and services available for consumption.

While it is apparent that the web of economic ties that links nations and their populations will continue to grow in the short run, its impact on the political interaction among nations is less obvious. Will these states lose their ability to choose freely from the slate of political strategies as they become more dependent upon one another for goods and services? If not, will these economic ties constrain a nation's ability to use force against other nations?

Typically when we think of economic ties among nations (whether we call it globalization, interdependence, or integration), the focus is on the welfare gains that result from opening market access and increasing trade. If economic interdependence influences the political behavior of states, it is worth digging a bit deeper to uncover the political ramifications of these economic relationships. Specifically, we need to understand how economic ties influence the decision to use military force. As world leaders continue to strive for increased economic linkages, the consequences for conflict may reshape the way we study world politics.

A Persistent Puzzle

Does economic interdependence lead to peace or conflict between nations? When two countries enter an economic relationship characterized by interdependence, are they constrained in their military behavior towards one another or are they adding one more source of disagreement over which conflict may emerge? Such questions have been of interest to scholars for centuries. Some have pursued these questions with hope that economic interdependence will help to extinguish interstate conflict. Immanuel Kant envisioned free trade between nations as one of the key ingredients to a peaceful world. Others have warned that such interaction merely provides one more reason for states to fight one another. Jean-Jacques Rousseau, for example, argued economic interaction would only bring discord and conflict. Modern scholarship still grapples with these opposing views.

The stakes for solving this puzzle are extremely high. In world politics, the manipulation of economic relationships for political reasons is neither new nor out of fashion. States frequently resort to the threat and the use of economic manipulation in an attempt to shape another state's foreign or domestic policy (e.g., the United States and Soviet Union in 1980). Just as frequently, it seems, we observe reluctance by states that appear to be in a position to use economic force and choose not to do so (for example, the United States and European Union decision to refrain from economic sanctions upon Russia for its civil war with Chechnya in

1999). What governs the willingness of nations to employ economic tools for political ends? Once employed, what determines the success of economic tools versus an escalating disagreement that may lead to more traditional (militarized) means of political conflict? Solving the interdependence-conflict puzzle will require answers to these two questions.

Existing approaches to this problem have focused on basic relationships, arguing that interstate economic interaction has a positive, negative, or non-effect on political conflict. A recent resurgence of work highlights the fact that despite the use of sophisticated data collection and research tools, the lack of consensus in the literature persists (Barbieri 1995, 1996, 2002; Mansfield and Pollins 2003; Oneal et al., 1996; Oneal and Russett 1997; Russett and Oneal 2001). Bruce Russett and John Oneal have integrated their work on trade and conflict into a broader assessment of the Kantian peace (2001). Their work shows strong evidence for the argument that trade between nations can lead to friendlier ties. Katherine Barbieri's work, on the other hand, demonstrates that often these trade ties can yield increased violence between nations. Who in this debate is on the right track?

Without taking anything away from the influence and accomplishments of this body of work, this empirical research may be incomplete, as we do not yet have a solid understanding of *how* interdependence influences conflict. Scholars have argued that the relationship between economic and political ties is more complex than a simple linear correlation between trade and conflict (Hirschman, 1945; Baldwin, 1980, 1985; Keohane and Nye, 1989). A causal theory of how and why economic interdependence and political conflict are related is still missing from our bag of scholarly tools, but the development of a causal theory may go a long way toward reshaping the way we study this relationship both theoretically and empirically. Forging this theoretical tool is the central task of this book.

This theoretical tool is useful not just for scholarly research, but for the policy world as well. Economic incentives have long been a favorite policy tool in the West for encouraging better political ties, especially when other factors like democracy are lacking. For example, one of the leading arguments for allowing China into the World Trade Organization (WTO) was that the increased economic interaction with the rest of the WTO members would foster cooperation in China's international relations and democratization within China's borders. Similar arguments bolster U.S. efforts to push market economic reforms in the former Soviet Union, as well as parallel efforts by the European Union to reform much of Eastern Europe.

These efforts typify the eagerness of the Western world to expand their access into new markets around the world. The political consequences of these efforts, however, are not fully understood. Specifically, it is important to be able to predict whether these investments will lead to political vulnerabilities for one or more nations due to these new economic ties. Even if the increased economic activity breeds a friendly, cooperative atmosphere (as argued by Russett and Oneal 2001), it may also unwittingly force a nation into a situation where it must yield to another to preserve its economic health. Knowing when economic interdependence will generate benign consequences vs. political vulnerabilities is a key goal of this book.

Setting the Agenda

The key to developing such a theory involves knowing when interdependence provides states the opportunity to link their economic ties to the political bargaining process. Using the interstate economic relationship as a political bargaining tool is the mechanism by which economic interdependence is tied to political behavior (Keohane and Nye, 1989). Interdependence influences the choices states make in both economic and political policy decisions. Identifying the mechanism states use to extract such bargaining power from their economic relationship will provide a framework to examine how interdependence influences political conflict. To this end, I undertake three tasks: (1) define the concept of economic interdependence as a function of exit costs driven by internal and systemic market factors, (2) develop a strategic model of the mechanism used by states to apply this economic interdependence as a political bargaining tool, and (3) empirically examine the implications derived from the theoretical model.

First, I define economic interdependence as a function of the potential exit costs states incur by breaking economic ties. These exit costs set apart interdependence from other qualities of interstate economic relations. Whereas economic interaction can be thought of simply as the transaction of goods or services between states, interdependence carries with it a connotation of constraint and a tangled web of commitments that are costly to break. Building from the platform that economic interdependence is driven by opportunity costs (Baldwin, 1980), I add to this concept by explicating the structural economic factors that generate these costs.

The factors governing exit costs can be found in the international system as well as internally within each state. At the systemic level, states are engaged in bilateral economic relationships within a global marketplace. The available opportunities for states to pursue alternate sources for goods and resources characterize the structure of the market. A market that contains many suppliers and consumers for a good, such as grain, presents states with a highly competitive environment, neutralizing the reliance of states upon each other to maintain their economic ties. A market with one or few suppliers of a good (monopoly power) or a shortage of buyers for a good (monopsony power) restricts the availability of alternate sources of economic interaction. Such markets provide far less competition, thus increasing the inefficiency of trade relationships and providing fewer options for states.

Market structure provides information about exit costs for states. This structural dimension is complemented by an internal source of exit costs: asset specificity. Asset specificity here refers to "the degree to which an asset can be redeployed to alternative users without sacrifice of production value" (Williamson, 1996: 59). As the assets that are involved in an economic relationship become more specific to that relationship, the costs of terminating or altering the terms of the relationship increase. These costs of exit represent the difference between interdependence and more fungible economic interaction.

Following this conceptual discussion, the second task of this book is to explore the strategic causal effects of the presence/absence of economic interdependence on interstate political behavior. I develop a strategic model of how interdependence can generate political leverage (via the threat of exit) as one state makes a demand upon another. I begin with the premise that two states are engaged in a relationship characterized by economic and political interaction. At least one of the states would like to alter the relationship in a way that is not desirable to the other (for example, one state seeks to claim or reclaim some disputed territory that the other state possesses). In this situation, a state (the "challenger") may see an opportunity to make a demand upon the other (the "target"), and it may choose to back up this demand with a threat of economic exit.

In response, the target state must decide whether to accept or reject the demand. If the target rejects the initial demand, then the state issuing the demand (the challenging state) must either retract its demand or persist and make good on its threat of economic exit. If the challenging state follows through on its threat and exits the economic relationship, both states will incur exit costs as they adapt to the new economic situation. Given this exit and the remaining demand by the challenger, the target state again chooses between accepting or rejecting the demand. If the target remains resistant to the challenger's demand, then the two states enter a more intense mode of conflict that is likely to involve more traditional dispute resolution tools such as the threat or use of military force. This abstract model captures the mechanism states use to translate economic interdependence into political bargaining power, providing a glimpse at the linkage between this interdependence and political conflict.

An analysis of this model predicts that exit costs can indeed deter challengers from seeking political demands that could otherwise lead to conflict. The costs of exit can also be used as leverage by a challenger to extract political demands, thereby generating low-level conflict between states that does not escalate to militarized levels. Finally, the model demonstrates that economic interdependence must be considered within the context of military power and the importance of political issues at stake. As these dimensions increase, states become more willing to bear the costs of economic exit and higher levels of militarized conflict ensue.

The third task of this book is to examine empirically the implications that emerge from the formal model and its analysis. To do this, I employ a multi-method approach with each method striking a different balance between external and internal validity. To capture the strategic process as well as predicted equilibrium behavior, three historical cases illustrate the analytical power of the model. These cases include the United States and South Africa from the mid-1960s to the early 1990s, the United States and China from 1989 to 1998, and Argentina and Great Britain during the Falkland Islands conflict of 1982. This method of using qualitative case histories to illustrate the structure and analytical results of the model provides the internal validity that is often necessary when exploring the empirical implications of game-theoretic models. Case selection issues and other research design problems, however, suggest that a more systematic analysis is also required.

The second stage of the empirical research attends to the need for a more systematic research design by employing a large-n analysis of the interdependence-conflict relationship with a sample of interstate dyads from the post-World War II period. Here I use measures of market power and trade as a proxy for interdependence and World Event Interaction Survey (WEIS) data to examine the impact of economic interdependence on interstate conflict. This approach facilitates more stringent research design requirements in terms of case selection and measurement validity, but these improvements come at the expense of internal content validity. The analyses provide support for the hypothesis that an increase in interdependence leads to an increase in low-level conflict as well as a decrease in high-level conflict. Together, the combination of case histories and statistical analysis suggest that the theoretical model captures the essence of the complex relationship between economic interdependence and interstate political conflict.

Before beginning this exploration, it is worthwhile for the reader to have access to a brief primer on the historical and current perspectives regarding the link between interstate economic and political behavior. Improvements in methodology and research design in the field of political science have renewed our attention to this linkage, but many of the theoretical arguments that guide our studies remain entrenched in the past. This imbalance is at least partially responsible for our inability to resolve the interdependence-conflict puzzle.

Perspectives

The study of the relationship between economics and politics in international relations is far from new. Previous research has been influenced deeply by the broader debate between realism and liberalism and their subsequent derivations. Liberal studies argue that economic ties reduce conflict. Realists emphasize the imbalances that are inherent in these ties, focusing on conflict rather than peace. Despite these long-standing debates, our grasp on the puzzle at hand remains tenuous at best, in part because the study of interdependence has been subsumed within these schools of thought. For example, McMillan (1997) identifies twenty empirical studies in a recent review of this literature. Ten of these studies support the liberal peace argument, four support the realist conflict argument, and six studies provide mixed results. While some of this disagreement can be attributed to differences in focus on a very complex research puzzle, the high degree of variance in findings is disturbing.

Below I briefly review the basic perspectives on the interdependence-conflict relationship. Before we continue with our empirical search for answers to this quandary, we need to step back and reevaluate the way we think about the issues at hand. Part of this evaluation will be to extract the study of this topic from the confines of the debate between liberalism and realism. These amorphous schools of thought are too cumbersome and too contentious to enable an objective consideration of the interdependence-conflict puzzle. Instead, the focus will be on the characteristics and structure of the relationship between economic ties and political behavior.

Figure 1.1 summarizes the theoretical and empirical connections represented in the literature regarding economic and political behavior. The exchange of resources between states is characterized in several ways. Scholars have focused on the amount (level) of economic exchange between states as a defining characteristic. Others have turned their attention to the salience of these levels of exchange, often by examining them relative to each state's gross domestic product. Still others have emphasized the asymmetry in the economic relationship as a source of change in the relative power between states.

Figure 1.1. Basic Relationships in the Literature

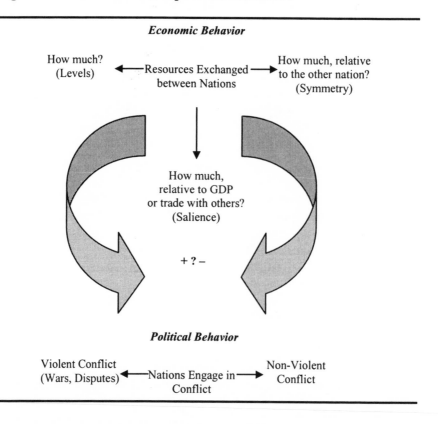

Economic Behavior

How much?
(Levels) ◀──Resources Exchanged──▶ How much, relative
          between Nations   to the other nation?
                                     (Symmetry)

How much,
relative to GDP
or trade with others?
(Salience)

+ ? –

Political Behavior

Violent Conflict   Non-Violent
(Wars, Disputes) ◀──Nations Engage in──▶   Conflict
                    Conflict

The presence or absence of conflict most frequently defines political behavior. This focus on conflict can vary drastically across studies. The most frequent approach is to restrict the analysis to the phenomena of war or less intense militarized conflict (militarized interstate disputes). A small number of studies also consider nonviolent forms of conflict such as diplomatic conflict. The impact of economic exchange upon political conflict behavior is typically argued to be one of three straightforward possibilities. One perspective argues that economic exchange has a negative impact on political conflict, leading to a more peaceful world. A contradictory body of research asserts that the relationship is positive, with economic exchange generating more conflictual behavior between states. Finally, a third argument posits that economic exchange is not sufficiently important to states to have any impact upon their decisions to engage in or avoid political conflict. I examine each of these three perspectives in turn. Each body of literature is diverse in its conceptualization of economic exchange and political conflict, but the logic that links the two phenomena together remains consistent.

Economic Exchange Decreases Political Conflict

> . . . the natural effect of commerce is to lead to peace. (Baron de Montesquieu, qtd. in Albert Hirschman, 1977: 80)

> The pacific benefits of interdependence are evident in all our tests. (John Oneal and Bruce Russett, 1997: 288)

One common perspective in the literature is the argument that economic interaction decreases the likelihood of conflict. Economic markets, if left alone by states to evolve and develop, will gradually interconnect states by economic means such as trade, thereby reducing the need for political boundaries and conflicts. Economic exchange will lead to security interests being replaced by economic interests. In turn, national interests become defined by the search for wealth. William Domke effectively captures the hopes of many scholars and policy makers when he argues that "the most potent challenge to the primacy of security is the pursuit of prosperity" (1988: 29).

Whether we rely on the classic international trade theories (such as Ricardo or Hecksher-Olin) or modern updates, these models fundamentally conclude that when two states specialize and trade in two goods, both states increase their overall consumption (Helpman and Krugman, 1985; Krugman and Obstfeld, 1991). This comparative advantage argument holds for all pairs of states, regardless of size and absolute advantages in the production of these goods.

This perspective traces back to Kant (1991 [1795]), who argued interdependence strengthens the peaceful ties between states by creating incentives to maintain a cooperative, lucrative environment for trade. International property rights and access rights facilitate profit and growth but they also require peace and cooperation between governments. As these economic ties grow stronger, so do the incentives to maintain a peaceful and cooperative international environment. As such, these incentives decrease the risk of international conflict.

Domke argues that the increase in wealth within each country resulting from trade generates a snowball effect on political conflict. Those who benefit from this increase in wealth put pressure upon their governments to seek peaceful means of resolving disputes with other countries. Preserving the flow of economic interaction through peace and diplomacy becomes a priority that can dwarf more traditional security concerns. Governments become more responsive to their citizens, and these citizens seek to protect their newfound prosperity by encouraging their governments to cooperate with other nations. Rosecrance (1986) provides a similar argument, associating increased trade with increased costs of fighting wars. As wars become more costly, alternative paths to pursuing political objectives become more appealing, but the mechanism by which trade alters state goals such that conflict becomes an outmoded and inefficient political tool remains unclear.

Domke (1988) also investigates the empirical relationship between interdependence and conflict on the systemic level. He proposes the hypothesis that greater levels of international trade for a state decreases the likelihood that the state will engage in war, and finds strong support for the negative relationship between international trade and war in an empirical investigation.[1] It is important to note that this hypothesis is not specific with respect to the three different types of economic interaction Domke identifies: interdependence, interconnectedness, and interpenetration. Interpenetration is defined as one nation's economic presence in another state. An ideal example of interpenetration is the multinational corporation (MNC), such as Japanese auto companies with manufacturing plants in the United States. Interconnectedness, on the other hand, is a less intense form of economic interaction, and presumably the economic ties are less binding than in the other two types of interaction. Domke does not decipher exactly which of these three types (or combination of the three) actually results in the support of the hypothesis, so it is difficult to rely on this study when specifically focusing on interdependence and war.

Edward Mansfield also argues that trade influences the patterns of war negatively, and like Domke he has difficulty in pinning down the precise relationship between trade and conflict. He finds that the level of international trade is inversely related to the onset of war. The causal explanation for this finding is wanting. Mansfield simply asserts that this result "probably reflects the fact that the expected costs of war are greater when the trade levels are higher, since the possibility that political conflict will stem the flow of commerce increases the trade-related opportunity costs of war" (1994: 27). This notion of expected costs of war being higher due to trade is the key to the logic of his theory, but no explanation is provided regarding how states determine these costs.

Mansfield empirically analyzes this relationship between international trade and war on the systemic level. He finds strong support for this negative relationship between trade and war, as well as support for the causal direction of trade as an influence of war. In particular, he concludes that international trade is inversely related to the incidence of wars involving major powers.

Solomon Polachek has been putting together pieces of this research puzzle for almost twenty years, and he continues to develop some of the most sophisticated arguments supporting the perspective that trade promotes peace. The argument is grounded in the notion of conflict as an inefficient drain on economic welfare. Trade relations emerge naturally through comparative advantage and resource allocations. Once this trade is in place, states will avoid conflict to preserve the resulting welfare improvements. He argues, "countries involved in *more* trade have on balance higher costs of conflict, and hence *ceteris paribus* are hypothesized to engage in *less* conflict" (1978: 73). He also briefly examines the notion that states possessing advantages or monopolies in trade markets enjoy a greater freedom to be hostile without worrying about reciprocation from trading partners. This would suggest that the market structure that provides context for the trade relationship is important when studying how trade affects conflict. His empirical tests focus on the dyadic level and the basic relationship between trade and conflict (as trade increases, conflict decreases). The results indicate strong support for the negative relationship between trade and conflict.

Polachek builds on this initial model and research significantly in several projects (1980, 1992, 1997). Most importantly, he continues to focus on the idea that not all trading relationships are the same. Along with Yuan-Ching Chang and John Robst, Polachek (1999) examines such issues as third-party conflict and market power. Using variations of the "friend of my friend is my friend" logic (Heider, 1946; Lee et al., 1994), the authors begin to examine how dyadic trade relations can have third-party effects on conflict. States with monopoly or monopsony power may experience a higher level of economic interdependence due to market failures. These extensions reinforce the need to go beyond the basic correlation analyses.

Sol Polachek and Judith McDonald (1992) extend their primary cost-benefit argument with a second proposition regarding trade and conflict, focusing on the inelasticity of the supply and demand of goods between two states. Elasticity refers to the ability of states to adjust the demand or supply of a good in the face of changes to its price. For example, when economic crisis hit Japan in the late 1990s, effectively raising the price of its imports, the Japanese were able to curb sharply their demand for apples imported from the United States.[2] Oil imports typify the opposite example. If a nation needs a certain quantity of oil—regardless of the price—to keep its production and transportation systems running, then this demand for oil is inelastic. Similarly, a nation that can adjust its exports of a commodity when prices increase or decrease has an elastic supply curve for that good. Polachek and McDonald aggregate this notion of elasticity across goods at the state level and argue:

> The more inelastic (elastic) an actor country's import demand
> and export supply to a target country, the smaller (larger) the
> amount of actor-to-target conflict. (1992: 277)

Again, assuming that conflict with another state results in a decrease in imports from and exports to that state, then one's inelasticity regarding these imports and exports compounds the costs incurred by fighting.

Recent studies by John Oneal and Bruce Russett (1997, 2001) provide additional support for the Kantian perspective. They examine politically relevant dyads from 1950 to 1985 and operationalize economic interdependence by measuring dyadic trade as a share of each state's GDP.[3] Using logistic regression in a binary time-series-cross-sectional research design, Oneal, Oneal, Maoz and Russett find, "Trade is a powerful influence for peace, especially among the war-prone, contiguous pairs of states" (1996: 11). Additional factors such as alliances, relative capabilities, and regime type do not alter this result. The pacific impact of interdependence is robust in their analysis.

There are several assumptions underlying this approach that are worth a closer look. The notion that two states can invariably enjoy greater wealth through trade than in autarky is indisputable. The assumption that the introduction of political conflict between trading states will reduce or eliminate their trade ties and thus their gains from trade, however, has recently come under fire. The basic argument underlying Polachek's work as well as the work done by Oneal and Russett is that the costs of fighting (including the loss of human life) are not strong enough to deter states from fighting. Costs incurred from the loss of trade, on the other hand, are enough to deter states from conflict.

Why should we expect the additional cost of losing trade ties to deter states from fighting? Do states engage in conflict despite the anticipated loss of economic ties? If so, what governs their decision to bear the added costs and fight or to preserve the economic relationship and remain peaceful? These questions go unanswered by this literature because it makes no attempt to understand how states weigh the costs and benefits of the options they face. Answers to these questions would require us to know not only how costly it would be to sever the economic ties, but also what is to be gained by fighting. There is an unspecified argument that states engage in a cost-benefit analysis of their available policy options regarding the use of force, but without an explicit understanding of this analysis we are unable to predict when the economic dimension will make the difference in preventing states from choosing conflict.

Recent methodological work by Beck, Katz, and Tucker (1998) calls the Oneal, et al., findings into question. By controlling for the autoregressive error (temporal history) in the empirical analysis, the negative relationship between economic interdependence and conflict becomes statistically insignificant. Beyond this methodological challenge, there are significant theoretical and empirical challenges to the fundamental logic underpinning this perspective. Stergios Skaperdas and Constantinos Syropoulos (1996) develop an economic model of trade and conflict that takes into account the presence of conflict and trading simultaneously. Skaperdas and Syropoulos find that in their economic model trade can persist in the face of conflict. The key to their results is that the incentive to trade does not go away in the face of conflict. They conclude that the argument that conflict eliminates trade is simply an artifact of extant theory. Using empirical tools rather than a theoretical approach, Katherine Barbieri and Jack Levy (1999) provide a similar critique of the assumption that trade halts in the face of conflict. They investigate the basic proposition that when we observe the incidence of conflict, we should also observe the cessation of trade. Surprisingly, they find that this fundamental relationship does not always hold. When conflict interrupts trade the long-term trading relationship is often undisturbed. Conflict only presents a short-term cost to states that engage in trade. It is a small leap to argue that such costs are worth the potential rewards of winning a political fight.

More importantly, these recent theoretical and methodological criticisms highlight the problem of assuming that economic costs result from conflict while ignoring the potential rewards that the conflict has to offer. In the next section, I examine the literature that presents an opposing view to the Kantian perspective. These scholars work from the premise that economic ties between countries can introduce new tensions and conflict.

Economic Exchange Increases Political Conflict

> Interdependence breeds not accommodation and harmony, but suspicion and incompatibility. (Stanley Hoffmann, 1965: 62)

> Extreme interdependence, whether symmetrical or asymmetrical, has the greatest potential for increasing the likelihood of conflict. (Katherine Barbieri, 1996: 29)

Not everyone agrees that economic ties between states will lead to peaceful relations. A competing approach focuses on the conflict generating effects of interdependence. Economic interdependence increases the ties and interaction between countries, thereby increasing the opportunity and likelihood of conflict. The key to this result is to focus on the *relative* welfare gains that result from economic interaction. Trade between two countries may generate an absolute increase in welfare for both states, but unless they have identical factors of production, one country will always gain more wealth relative to the other. The asymmetrical distribution of economic factors generates economic inequalities between states that may translate into power inequalities. The threat of these emerging power inequalities leads to state hostility. Robert Gilpin (1987) focuses on uneven growth in the global economy and its negative consequences for peace. This uneven growth leads to structural changes in the world economy. As this relative change generates winners and losers, nations respond with political conflict.

Katherine Barbieri (1995, 2002) finds empirical support for the argument that economic interdependence increases political conflict. She approaches the economic interdependence-conflict puzzle from a dyadic perspective using large-n, empirical methods. In a study that examines roughly 70,000 dyads over a period of 115 years, Barbieri breaks down interdependence into *salience* and *symmetry* dimensions. The concept of salience reflects the "combined importance of the relationship for both partners" (1995: 75). It is a multiplicative measure that is structurally based on the ratio of one country's trade with another country compared to its overall trade.[4] Symmetry, on the other hand, is a measure that compares the relative dependencies of the two countries to each other for each dyad. Thus, "symmetry represents a dyadic attribute of the relationship, based on the degree to which partners are similarly dependent upon the relationship" (1995: 76). Interdependence is measured by interacting the two dimensions of salience and symmetry.

Barbieri concludes that highly salient economic interdependence leads to an increase in militarized disputes, but it has little impact on wars. Mutual (symmetrical) dependence increases the likelihood of peace, but intensity increases the likelihood of conflict. Overall, her results support the conflictual consequence of interdependence, as she argues that "gains from trade associated with expanded trade do not appear to create a sufficient incentive to make conflict less likely" (1995: 227). Her research precedes and is very similar to Oneal, et al. (1996) and Oneal and Russett (1997), yet her findings contradict their position that interdependence leads to decreased conflict. While the differences in spatio-temporal domain and operationalization are in part responsible for this variance in findings, the stark difference in the two positions is troublesome.

Similarly, Mark Gasiorowski (1986) looks at trade levels and war and finds that interdependence results in an increase in conflict. He claims "international interdependence, defined as a relationship involving real or potential costs, produces increased international conflict" (1986: 36). He then differentiates between costly and beneficial interdependence. The presence of costly interdependence increases the likelihood of conflict while the beneficial form decreases conflict. Maximizing the benefits and minimizing the costs of interdependence can lead to peace and stability in the international system. This discussion of costs versus benefits in interdependence provides a glimpse at the qualitative difference between interdependence and interaction. Interaction consists only of the benefits of trade, while interdependence carries both the costs and benefits of the economic ties. It is unclear, however, what constitutes beneficial versus costly trade for Gasiorowski.

There are some peculiar similarities between those who argue that economic exchange is positively or negatively related to political conflict. Both sides tend to approach the puzzle with the same research tools, often using the same data in their analyses. Small changes in research design and case selection may contribute to their disagreements, but a more serious problem lies in an insufficient theoretical focus. While the literature has come a long way toward improving on research design and empirical analysis, the theoretical relationship between economic exchange and political conflict remains underdeveloped. This lack of focus in the theory is also prevalent in the body of research that argues that economic ties have little or no impact on political conflict.

Economic Exchange is Irrelevant to Political Conflict

> What does it mean then to say that the world is an increasingly interdependent one in which all nations are constrained, a world in which all nations lose control? Very little. (Kenneth Waltz, 1979: 153)

The third perspective that is common in this literature asserts that economic exchange is irrelevant to the level of political conflict in the international system. There are two strains to this side of the debate: the classic position taken by structural realists and a more recent set of arguments set forth by rationalist (rational choice) scholars. The first group, the structural realists, maintains the distribution of power in the international system is the key factor in determining peace and conflict. Buzan (1984) asserts that the pacific and conflictual arguments regarding international economics are moot for the simple reason that the structural military relationship among states completely dominates interstate political behavior. Economics may influence international relations at the margin, but the fundamental character of peace and conflict will not be determined by these subordinate concerns. Focusing on the structural effects of the distribution of power provides an elegant and parsimonious yet powerful way of studying global outcomes.

Gilpin also downplays the causal impact of economics on politics:

> The major point to be made in these matters is that trade and other economic relations are not themselves critical to the establishment of either cooperative or conflictual international relations. No generalizations on the relationship of economic interdependence and political behavior appear possible. At times economic intercourse can moderate and at others aggravate these relations. . . . In general, the character of international relations and the question of peace or war are determined primarily by the larger configurations of power and strategic interest among both great and small powers in the system. (1987: 58)

This statement counters Gilpin's earlier prediction of conflict from economic interaction. Gilpin refers to the impact of change in the economic relationship between two states in the first quote, but refers to the static relationship between economic interdependence and conflict in the second. His conflicting arguments are a good example of how many scholars find it difficult to pin down the relationship between economic exchange and political conflict. The relationship is almost certainly more complex than any of these three perspectives can recognize. The next section investigates some of the recent attempts by scholars to reveal some of the complexities of the interdependence-conflict puzzle.

More recently, an interesting critique of the existence of a causal link between interdependence and conflict has emerged from the rationalists' camp (Morrow 1999, Gartzke 2003). The challenge identified by Morrow is simple but powerful: those who are involved in economic interactions anticipate conflicts between nations and adjust their behavior before a crisis develops. This adjustment may involve finding alternative sources of economic exchange either at home or abroad, for example. As a result they do not pay the costs of severed economic activity when a crisis develops. Without this cost there is no pressure placed upon governments to avoid the crisis, which removes the causal mechanism that links economic interdependence and international conflict.

Morrow's challenge raises the burden of proof for scholars who argue that interdependence increases or diminishes conflict. In this book I embrace this challenge by focusing on a theory of economic interdependence that hinges on the ability of markets and firms to adjust to changes in the international economic and political environment.

The second challenge from the rationalists comes from both Morrow (1999, 2003) and Gartzke (2003), and it centers on the role of information and conflict. This line of reasoning centers on the current state of wisdom in the study of conflict that suggests wars only result between nations when these actors are unable to credibly convey the critical information about their willingness to accept a negotiated settlement. The complexity of world politics affords nations the luxury of private information: nations are unable to accurately assess the degree to which their opponents are serious about a dispute or a particular bargaining position. The existence of this private information leads to the incentive to misrepresent one's own position in a dispute (e.g., bluffing, etc.). This misrepresentation, and the inability of states to convince their opponents in a crisis that they are *not* bluffing, can lead to war.

Given the critical dimension of information in determining the occurrence of war, any theory of economic interdependence and war should focus on how this interdependence affects the problem of information that leads to war. To date, such a theory does not exist. This opens the door for Gartzke's claim that scholars who predict a pacifying relationship between interdependence and conflict (the classic liberals) are lucky (2003). They are lucky because they have accurately identified this correlation, but their work misses the mark because the correlation is spurious (both phenomena are caused by something else).

In this case, Gartzke suggests that international economic markets may be doing all the work. In the aggregate, international markets can provide accurate estimates of private information, thereby having a real effect on the information problem that can lead to war. Here it is important to identify the broader liberal theory of the state, which is designed to limit the ability of the state to interfere with this process. Thus the interaction of international economic markets and democratic/capitalist governments can generate a meaningful constraint on the occurrence of conflict.

The ideas underlying these criticisms are very important to our future understanding of the interdependence-conflict relationship. That said, it is easy to overestimate the ability of markets or any other economic unity (such as the firm) to inform and adjust quickly. Just as friction interferes with our basic models of gravity and motion in physics, markets are "sticky" and information does not get cleared immediately. Unlike the field of physics, however, the "stickiness" of markets and firms with respect to their ability to adapt to change and the anticipation of change is unidentified (simply put, the sources of friction are much easier to identify and much less complex than the sources of stickiness in world politics). If markets and firms move too slowly, then their ability to anticipate and thus compensate for conflict may not be sufficient, thus restoring their interest in pressuring governments to use restraint (and restoring the causal mechanism that links interdependence and conflict).

While I do not introduce the problem of private information into the theory of interdependence and conflict developed in chapter 3, I do consider the costs of adjustment imposed by the structure of the market to be paramount to the existence of economic *interdependence* as opposed to economic *interaction*. In a sense I have shifted the role of the market to the existence of interdependence rather than focus on its role in tying interdependence to conflict. The following two chapters shed further light on this distinction.

Complex Linkages: Expectation, Domestic Politics, and Bargaining

The restrictions imposed by each of the three perspectives discussed above have proven to be too constraining for many students of world politics. Recently scholars have sought to expand our understanding of the relationship between economic exchange and political behavior. One such extension is the notion that future expectations of trade benefits are critical to the decision to fight or maintain trade ties (Copeland, 1996). For example, a trade relationship that is deteriorating and shows little potential of rebounding will be easier to break than weak trade ties in a relationship for which growth in trade is expected. Copeland also incorporates an essential extension to the analysis of interdependence and conflict: he argues that when states consider the decision to go to war and thus sever their economic ties, they consider the costs of trade interruption within the context of the potential gains from war.

Domestic factors, such as domestic institutional structure, have also emerged as contributing factors to the relationship between economic ties and political behavior (Papayoanou, 1996; Oneal and Russett, 1997). The emphasis here is on how democratic institutions are more sensitive than authoritarian structures to the potential costs of losing gains from trade. Whether the conclusion favors a positive, negative, or absent linkage between trade and conflict, the basic premise of the deterrence of conflict for the sake of maintaining wealth from trade remains constant.

Not all of the studies recognizing the pacific effects of economic ties rely on this liberalist premise. Keohane and Nye (1989) renewed the quintessential argument established by Hirschman (1945) that economic interdependence is a source of political power for nations. Rather than adhering to rather utopian themes of the pacific impact of economic relations, this approach is more concerned with the way economic interdependence generates economic power that may influence political bargaining between states. While states are not moving toward a world of pure cooperation, they may choose to rely on their economic power rather than military power to resolve both economic and political differences. Keohane and Nye are quick to point out that this perspective does not assume that economic exchange leads to Kant's vision of perpetual peace:

We do not limit the term, *interdependence* to situations of mutual benefit. Such a definition would assume that the concept
is only useful analytically where the modernist view of the
world prevails: where threats of military force are few and
levels of conflict are low. (1989: 9, emphasis in original)

Thus, the ties between states generate bargaining opportunities that can
have both pacific and conflictual consequences.

Keohane and Nye characterize interdependence in two ways: (1) by
making a qualitative distinction between sensitivity and vulnerability in
this interdependence, and (2) by focusing on the symmetry of the joint
dependence between states. They argue that asymmetrical, vulnerable
interdependence generates a new set of constraints and incentives beyond
those created by relative military power. They do not argue that economic influences dominate military concerns, but they do claim that the
costs associated with military foreign policy options may make economic
bargaining options preferable.

These extensions demonstrate that the three basic relationships (positive, negative, zero) are insufficient lenses to decipher the interdependence-conflict puzzle. The relationship between economic and political
interaction at the state level is far more complex than any linear relationship can capture. This relationship is far too broad and complex for one
book to encompass. Attempts such as Gilpin's to assess the entire relationship have resulted in fuzzy terminology and elusive causal linkages.
Rather than add to the confusion that pervades this topic and weighs
down our ability to decipher the puzzle, the agenda of this book is to
identify one particular causal link between economic exchange and political behavior.

Outline of the Book

Chapter 2 identifies the concepts of economic interdependence and political conflict as they will be used throughout this book. Drawing on
transaction cost economics, I introduce the context of market structure
and asset specificity in the basic conceptualization of economic interdependence (Williamson, 1975; North, 1990). Interdependence is defined
by the costs incurred by each state in a dyad to remove itself from bilateral economic ties. These costs of exit are in turn a function of the market in terms of the availability of substitutable goods and buyers of
goods, as well as adaptation costs associated with restructuring the transactions required to satisfy economic demand. Low levels of exit costs

generate little or no need for political interaction between states. As exit costs increase or become asymmetrical across the dyad, opportunities arise in which one state can make political demands on the other by threatening to exit the economic relationship, thereby imposing the costs of exit on the other state. At very high levels of exit costs, a state may be motivated to engage in conflict with the other state in the hopes of restructuring the economic relationship to diminish the potential costs of exit.

After establishing economic interdependence as a function of exit costs, chapter 3 turns to the question of how this interdependence generates political behavior. This second leg of the research agenda ultimately must be answered empirically. If we continue to proceed with empirical investigations without addressing the conceptual and theoretical problems plaguing this literature, we will make little progress towards resolving this debate. More importantly, we will continue to mistakenly operationalize the concept of economic interdependence, and thus fail to assess properly both its presence and its impact on interstate conflict.

Consequently, I develop a model that focuses on the strategic problems that arise when demands are made based on economic threats of exit. The analysis shows that exit costs can result in one state successfully compelling another to concede to demands, signifying low level conflict that does not escalate. This ability to coerce is mitigated by such factors as the value states place upon the issues at stake in the demand and the military power each state can employ in the event of militarized conflict. Finally, exit costs for the state wishing to make a demand can constrain this state from doing so, provided that the other state does not face similar costs. Thus, the model indicates that three possible paths of behavior emerge from the different configurations of interdependence within a dyad. The model also suggests that directionality is more important than symmetry and that intensity or salience in interdependence is only relevant when placed in the context of the broader political relationship.

Chapters 4 and 5 explore the empirical implications of the formal analysis. Chapter 4 illustrates the implications derived in the equilibrium analysis of the exit model in chapter 3. Three case histories are employed to represent the equilibria revealed in an analysis of the exit model. The case of China and the United States from post-Tiananmen Square (1989) to 1998 illustrates the ability of a challenger state (China) to extract demands from a seemingly economically superior target state (the United States) by leveraging exit costs. On the other hand, examining the United States and South Africa during the Apartheid era demonstrates how exit costs can constrain even superpowers from making demands. Finally, the case of Argentina and Great Britain during the Falkland Islands conflict of 1982 illustrates the limits of economic interdependence given the context of the issues at stake in the potential dispute. The three cases serve to flesh out the abstract exit model, as well as to demonstrate the plausibility of each equilibrium path. They also reveal the limits of the exit model and the consequences of imposing assumptions upon information and treating entire nations as unitary actors.

Chapter 5 complements this qualitative analysis with a more systematic but abstract large-n analysis. I examine a sample of dyads using statistical methods to show how changes in economic interdependence result in changes in the interstate political behavior. The results support the hypotheses derived from the exit model. Chapter 6 concludes with an overview of what has emerged from the formal and empirical analyses, and suggests directions for future research.

Notes

1. Domke argues that we can test hypotheses in the state level of analysis and use the results as a critique of systemic arguments.
2. Specifically, apples imported from the state of Washington in the United States are considered a delicacy in Japan. Apple growers in the United States, on the other hand, had a harder time finding new markets for their goods.
3. Politically relevant dyads consist of all pairs of states that are contiguous or contain at least one major power (Oneal and Russett, 1997: 273).
4. The functional forms of salience and symmetry will be examined in more detail in chapter 2.

2
Concepts:
Sorting the Pieces of the Puzzle

Where there are reciprocal . . . costly effects of transactions, there is interdependence. (Robert Keohane and Joseph Nye, 1989: 9)

A country menaced with an interruption of trade with a given country has the alternative of diverting its trade to a third country; by doing so it evades more or less completely the damaging consequences of the stoppage of its trade with one particular country. (Albert Hirschman, 1945: 29)

Chapter 1 illustrates how scholars commonly impose a rough equivalence between economic interdependence and trade. Trade is the form of economic exchange that is the most intuitive to us, so this substitution is not surprising. It is much easier to grasp the phenomena of trading grain and oil than it is to wrestle with concepts such as market power or capital flows. Data on trade is also widely available for a large set of countries over a long period of time, making it an easy choice for empirical analysis. As easy and intuitive as it may be to focus on trade, however, this often causes the scholar to overlook key information about the context within which trade and other forms of economic exchange take place. Specifically, the global economic markets within which states and other economic actors interact shape this context. Domestic factors are also important. They determine a state's demand for goods and services, as well as its ability to adapt to changing global markets.

This context is what separates economic interdependence from other forms of exchange. Failing to consider these global and domestic factors risks grouping together dyads that are enjoying trade within a free and competitive market with pairs of nations that are trading in part because they are constrained by market imperfections or failures (i.e., a monopoly or scarcity of goods). By confusing interdependence with high economic activity that would be relatively costless to change, we are unable to assess the impact of economic interdependence on interstate conflict decisions.

In this chapter, I develop the concepts of economic interdependence and interstate conflict for the purposes of this study. After exploring the existing definitions of interdependence, I focus the reader's attention to the role of opportunity costs. These costs are a product of imperfect markets and asset specificity. I do not argue that qualities such as intensity and symmetry are not useful tools to understand interdependence, but they become relevant only when the fungibility of the economic ties between two states degenerates and the costs of exiting the relationship are high. High levels of economic activity may not signal interdependence if both parties are able to access new markets at home and abroad in the event of a disruption in trade. On the other hand, low levels of economic activity may mask the existence of interdependence that is driven by monopoly or monopsony power.

Conceptual development in the area of interstate conflict is considerably more extensive and rigorous. Given this relative clarity, the remaining task will be to specify the range and character of political conflict encompassed in this book. Chapter 1 demonstrated that research on the relationship between international economics and political conflict has been diverse, as scholars focus on their own piece of a very large problem. Several scholars have focused on war as the phenomenon to be explained (Domke, 1988; Mansfield, 1994). Others have employed the broader concept of Militarized Interstate Disputes (Barbieri, 1996; Oneal and Russett, 1997) as well as a broader range of activity encompassing both conflict and cooperation (Polachek, 1997).

I argue below that violent conflict such as disputes and wars should be distinguished from nonviolent conflict. The absence of military violence in a dispute does not always imply cooperation between nations. To capture this broader range of behavior, I specify a definition of conflict that accounts for states that use nonviolent means to resolve their disputes. Care is taken, however, to preserve the distinction between nonviolent (low-level) and violent (high-level) conflict. Thus, the traditional focus on violent conflict is not diluted by lumping war and disputes with diplomatic protests and sanctions, but I am able to consider these less intense types of events when examining the impact of interdependence.

Identifying Economic Interdependence

> . . . interconnectedness is not the same as interdependence. The effects of transactions on interdependence will depend on the constraints, or costs, associated with them. . . . Where there are reciprocal . . . costly effects of transactions, there is interdependence. Where interactions do not have significant costly effects, there is simply interconnectedness. This distinction is vital if we are to understand the *politics* of interdependence. (Robert Keohane and Joseph Nye, 1989: 9, emphasis in original)

Whenever there are a plethora of terms used interchangeably to describe a phenomenon, it is a clear sign of our failure to conceptualize and organize this phenomenon to the satisfaction of the scholarly discipline. In the study of economics and politics, economic behavior between states is not alone in suffering from this conceptual muddiness. Indeed, placing two introductory political science texts side by side and comparing them would reveal that clarity and consistency are not characteristics that are readily applicable to many of the concepts we study.

Few concepts, however, suffer from the crowd of terms employed to characterize economic behavior between nations. Terms that have been preempted by the word *economic* and assigned to represent some form of economic behavior include: ties, interaction, relations, linkages, internationalization, interpenetration, integration, dependence, and, of course, interdependence. This list reflects our attempts to grasp the variety of economic behavior between states. This diversity of concepts is not surprising, but it can pose problems for research. In this section I focus on existing definitions of economic interdependence and how these definitions separate this phenomenon from the broader class of economic interaction.

First to Market: Hirschman's Study of Power and Trade

In his work *National Power and the Structure of Foreign Trade*, Hirschman (1945) sets out to understand the ways in which trade relationships can be translated by nations into power and influence. His interests lie in examining trade as an instrument of national power, or the "power of coercion which one nation may bring to bear upon other nations" (1945: 13). As such, his primary goal is to reveal how and why coercion can emerge from trade relations. He asserts:

> If A wants to increase its hold on B, C, D, etc., it must create a situation in which these countries would do *anything* in order to retain their foreign trade with A. (1945: 17, emphasis in original)

In identifying the required economic context to generate this situation of influence for state A, Hirschman keys in almost immediately on the multinational perspective that is essential to the concept of interdependence:

> Such a situation arises when it is extremely difficult and onerous for these countries: 1) to dispense entirely with the trade they conduct with A, or 2) to replace A as a market and source of supply with other countries. (1945: 17)

The first condition requires that the trading relationship involve the transaction of non-trivial goods and services, such that the cost to A's trading partners of going without these goods and services is high enough to ensure compliance with A's demands.[1] The second condition involves the ability of A's trading partners to find alternative markets to replace their relationship with A in the event that A engages in coercive practices.

This discussion of market structure is what separates Hirschman from other studies. With few exceptions (see Polachek and McDonald, 1992; Polachek, 1997; and Polachek, Chang and Robst, 1999), recent research has proceeded (implicitly) under the assumption that high levels of trade activity between two nations indicates that both of Hirschman's conditions are in place. Instead of examining market structure, their concern has been primarily with identifying the degree to which the interruption of bilateral trade is costly to one or both states. This focus on trade activity is inconsistent with Hirschman's discussion of the importance of market context.

It appears that the conceptual progress prior to the 1980s has been lost in pursuit of measurement. For example, in a review of the state of the literature on the concept of economic interdependence, Baldwin (1980) argues for a greater reliance on Hirschman's work and defines this concept as reciprocal opportunity costs.[2] The opportunity costs involved are what each state would face in the event of a termination of the economic relationship. That these costs are reciprocal is what separates dependence and interdependence. As such, these costs are a function of the dyadic economic relationship *and* the possible alternatives to that relationship. It is this second piece of the puzzle that has lost its way in current research. In the next section I investigate the contribution by Keohane and Nye to this topic. Their conceptualization of interdependence is largely an extension of Hirschman's, and their discussion of vulnerability persists as the standard definition of economic interdependence in the field.

Sensitivity versus Vulnerability

Keohane and Nye provide what has become the most influential conceptual discussion of interdependence to date. They argue that if dependence indicates a reliance upon external forces that significantly affect a state's behavior and autonomy, then interdependence is a *shared* reliance between two states. Keohane and Nye identify interdependence as

> . . . characterized by reciprocal effects among countries. . . . Where there are reciprocal (although not necessarily symmetrical) costly effects of transactions, there is interdependence. (1989: 8-9)

Interdependence involves both costs and benefits. Benefits must exist because they are the incentives for states to move toward interdependence. Costs emerge once ties between states are made and these costs are directly related to the act of breaking these ties. Interdependence is distinguished from interconnectedness because it involves a mutual dependence between states.

Interdependence can emerge from interconnectedness if states become dependent upon these transactions. When this happens, changes in the structure or presence of these transactions would result in costs for at least one of the states involved. For example, if State A begins to trade with State B and begins importing oil, ties of interconnectedness emerge. If State A begins to rely on the imported oil as a source of energy to run its industrial economy, it develops a dependency upon State B. If the oil exporting state (B) becomes dependent either upon the resulting cash flow from the importing country (A) or any other good or service that the oil importing country may provide, then interdependence occurs. The benefits of the imported oil or the exported cash remain, but now a sense of cost exists in the potential for one or both states to alter these transactions. Interdependence does not assume symmetry, but it cannot occur unless there is some degree of dependence and cost on both sides of a dyadic relationship.

Keohane and Nye discuss interdependence in terms of two distinctive characteristics: *sensitivity* and *vulnerability*.[3] *Sensitivity* refers to the immediacy and initial intensity of costs that another state can impose by altering the interdependent relationship. Sensitivity involves the acute reaction costs incurred by a state due to unexpected changes. *Vulnerability*, on the other hand, is defined by a state's ability to compensate and rebound from costs incurred as a result of policy changes from another state. Thus, if a state is immediately and intensely affected by a hike in oil prices by a trading partner, that state is sensitive to those changes. If, however, it is able to compensate quickly for the price hike by either seeking alternate sources of energy or alternate sources of oil, then the state is not vulnerable to such economic manipulations. On the other hand, if the nation's economy is paralyzed by the oil hike and is unable to change its behavior to compensate for the costs, that state is both sensitive and vulnerable to the state providing the oil.

Cooper (1985) reiterates the conceptual distinctions between sensitivity and vulnerability and labels them as the two competing definitional forms of interdependence. Vulnerability interdependence concerns the costs of doing without transactions in the event that economic ties break. These costs refer to the remaining costs states face after they have adapted to the new situation to the best of their ability. Sensitivity interdependence, on the other hand, refers to the short-term adjustment costs states make in response to foreign events "under conditions of normal economic activity" (1985: 1197). As such, sensitivity interdependence involves the costs of *being in* an economic relationship with another country, while vulnerability interdependence refers to the costs of *getting out* of such a relationship.

Keohane and Nye make an important contribution, but one question remains. How do these costly effects manifest themselves? Only by identifying the causal factors of these opportunity or exit costs can we begin to identify interdependence systematically. Baldwin (1980) is correct to focus political scientists toward vulnerability in interdependence and opportunity costs. Without an understanding of the conditions that generate these costs, however, scholars have had a difficult time identifying vulnerability in a systematic fashion. Recent research focuses on interdependence as a variable in large-n quantitative research. Abstract conceptual discussions are shed in favor of variables that facilitate replicable empirical study. The next section examines these variables and evaluates their success in capturing the information required to identify economic interdependence.

Salience and Symmetry

Barbieri (1995) cites the elusiveness of vulnerability as motivation for a different approach. She also disaggregates interdependence into two dimensions, but reduces sensitivity and vulnerability into one dimension: *salience*. Salience refers to the "importance of the trading relationship, relative to other trading relationships" (1995: 71). The salience of trade for one state in a trading dyad need not be identical to the salience for its trading partner. For example, Canada's trade with the Unites States represents a far greater proportion of Canada's total trade than it does for the United States. Rather than relying on a qualitative difference between sensitivity and vulnerability (the line between the two appears to be blurred to say the least) salience in interdependence is classified as a continuous concept. Lower levels of salience are analogous to sensitivity, and higher levels are similar to vulnerability.

The second key dimension in Barbieri's treatment of interdependence is *symmetry* in state dependence. Recognizing that the salience of the economic relationship can vary within the dyad, symmetry captures the relative balance of economic interdependence. At one extreme, perfect symmetry exists when both states are equally dependent upon one another. Perfect asymmetry occurs when one state is completely dependent upon its trading partner, but this partner has almost no dependence on the first state.[4] Keohane and Nye also address symmetry, arguing that it is the existence of asymmetry in economic interdependence that can be a source of economic power for the less dependent state. They are far less rigorous, however, in their specification.

Barbieri calculates interdependence using a three-stage process. First, she establishes the relative importance of the dyadic trading relationship for each state compared to their overall trade (in both cases, imports and exports). Given two states, State I and State J, $TradeShare_{ij}$ represents the economic exchange between States I and J relative to all of State I's economic partners. The concept is directional within the dyad, and is obtained using equation 2.1 where $DyadicTrade_{ij}$ is the amount of imports and exports exchanged between State I and State J, and *Total-Trade_i* is the aggregate imports and exports for State I with all of its trading partners:

$$TradeShare_{ij} = \frac{DyadicTrade_{ij}}{TotalTrade_i}. \tag{2.1}$$

Scores for this measure range from zero to one, with zero representing no imports or exports between State I and State J, and a score of one indicating that State I conducts all of its international trade only with State J. Given this base proportion of trade, she then calculates the salience of the interdependence within the dyad. To do this, she multiplies the *TradeShare* proportions for both states, and then takes the square root of the product, as in equation 2.2:

$$Salience_{ij} = \sqrt{TradeShare_{ij} * TradeShare_{ji}}. \tag{2.2}$$

Using this measure, she links the two nations' trade dependencies such that a low level of dependence for either state reduces the overall salience of the relationship. Out of the two directional *TradeShare* scores, one nondirectional salience score is generated for the dyad.

In the second stage, the symmetry of the two trade dependencies is assessed with equation 2.3:

$$Symmetry_{ij} = 1 - \left| TradeShare_{ij} - TradeShare_{ji} \right|. \tag{2.3}$$

A symmetry score of one indicates that State$_i$ and State$_j$ are perfectly symmetrical, while a score near zero indicates the most asymmetrical relationship that is possible. Like its salience score counterpart, the symmetry score is dyadic and nondirectional. The third stage in the calculation of interdependence is to combine the two dimensions of the economic relationship into one measure:

$$Interdependence_{ij} = Salience_{ij} * Symmetry_{ij}. \tag{2.4}$$

The two dimensions interact to generate interdependence. Interdependence is at its highest when both states rely heavily upon the other for their trade needs such that salience and symmetry scores are both near one. Lower levels of either salience or symmetry will drive down the overall interdependence of the dyad, and high levels of both dimensions are needed for the highest levels of interdependence.

Oneal and Russett (1997) define interdependence similarly to Barbieri. They first identify the trade dependence of State I on State J. Rather than examining the dyadic trade activity relative to overall trade,

Oneal and Russett assess State I's dependence on State J relative to State I's gross domestic product, using equation 2.5:

$$Depend_{ij,t} = \frac{(X_{ij,t} + M_{ij,t})}{GDP_{i,t}}.$$ (2.5)

$Depend_{ij,t}$ is a directional score for State I with respect to State J. $X_{ij,t}$ denotes exports from State I to State J at time t, and $M_{ij,t}$ denotes imports to State I from State J at time t. The only real difference between this measure and Barbieri's measure is the use of Gross Domestic Product information in the denominator.[5] Oneal and Russett consider the economic exchange between I and J relative to each state's overall economic output. They then examine each state's dependence independently, identifying which state has a greater dependence within the dyadic relationship.

Table 2.1 summarizes the explicit conceptualizations of interdependence. Although the work by Oneal and Russett and Barbieri exceeds the clarity and rigor of Keohane and Nye's discussion of interdependence, the three approaches have one thing in common. They all focus on how to interpret or measure the intensity and balance of these costs for pairs of states and assume away the problem of identifying what drives opportunity costs. Unfortunately, Baldwin's 1980 conclusion that "from a conceptual standpoint the period since 1968 has contributed very little to thinking about international interdependence" still holds true today (489). We still require a definition of economic interdependence that delineates the source of opportunity costs. The next section sets forth a definition of interdependence based upon the costs associated with a state exiting an economic relationship with another state. These opportunity costs of exit, or exit costs, are driven by factors at the systemic and domestic levels. The result is a working definition of interdependence that facilitates more focused and valid research.

Table 2.1. Concepts of Economic Interdependence (EI)

Author(s)	Conceptual Definition of EI
Hirschman (1945)	EI is a function of the alternatives states face with respect to economic ties. A lack of alternatives in the marketplace leads to interdependence. A lack of diversity in trading partners and a high degree of international trade as a proportion of a state's total economy both exacerbate the problem.
Baldwin (1980)	EI results when mutual cost-benefits of economic linkage in interstate relationships exceed alternatives. EI manifests itself as reciprocal opportunity costs. These costs refer to severing existing economic ties.
Keohane and Nye (1989), Cooper (1985)	EI involves mutual costly ties. Sensitivity refers to short-term costs of adaptation to severing economic ties or costs associated with maintaining the relationship; vulnerability refers to long-term costs that occur despite adaptation when the economic relationship is severed.
Barbieri (1995)	EI is a function of the interaction of trade salience and symmetry between two states. Trade salience is a function of the total trade between two states as a proportion of each state's total trade with the international system. Symmetry is a function of the balance of the importance of trade between the two states.
Oneal and Russett (1997)	Broken down into directional dependence, which is a function of the trade between the two states as a proportion of GDP for each state.

Exit Costs and Economic Interdependence

> To trace the effects that follow from inequalities, one has to unpack the word "interdependent" and identify the varying mixtures of relative dependence for some nations and of relative independence for others. (Kenneth Waltz, 1979: 153)

To define economic interdependence, I begin by returning to the work of Hirschman and Baldwin to emphasize the role of opportunity costs. The opportunity costs of exiting an economic relationship drive interdependence, and Hirschman's discussion of the role of the marketplace is critical in determining the origin of these costs. To illustrate the importance of context, consider a story that typifies our treatment of interdependence and highlights the need for a better understanding of its underlying factors. Baldwin (1980: 483) cites the following story by Sir Norman Angell to demonstrate what he considered to be the fundamental character of interdependence:

> The boat was leaky, the sea heavy, and the shore a long way off. It took all the efforts of the one man to row, and of the other to bail. If either had ceased both would have drowned. At one point the rower threatened the bailer that if he did not bail with more energy he would throw him overboard; to which the bailer made the obvious reply that, if he did, he (the rower) would certainly drown also. And as the rower was really dependent upon the bailer, and the bailer upon the rower, neither could use force against the other. (Angell, 1914: 17)

From this story we get an intuitive sense that these two men rely upon one another for their survival. A close examination of the situation, however, reveals a need for missing information required to decipher *why* the two men are interdependent.

The first missing piece of information is that there are only two men on the boat. This information is implicitly built into the sentence, "If either had ceased both would have drowned." If there were more people on the boat then each man would have the option of finding other men or women to row and bail, thereby relieving the interdependence of the two men. With only the two men, the markets for rowers and bailers are monopolistic (with each man holding a monopoly over his skill). Thus, implicit in this story is the fact that there are only two people on the boat.

The second missing piece deals with man's ability to adapt to changing circumstances. Implicit in this story is the assumption that if one man was removed from the boat, the other man could not successfully split his energy between rowing and bailing to survive. Again, this must be the case for the following sentence to hold true: "It took all the efforts of the one man to row, and of the other to bail." In other words, neither man is capable of adapting his assets to the situation if the other man jumped ship.

When first reading Angell's story, we are hard pressed to imagine the need for more information to conclude the two men are interdependent. Even in this extreme case, however, we find that we need more information about the potential costs that each man faces in the absence of the other. This information problem only gets worse when we consider the complex nature of world politics. Seemingly trivial information now becomes more important. Assuming states do not have viable alternative trading partners leads to erroneous predictions about interdependence. Similarly, we cannot assume that a state is unable to adapt internally to a loss of economic exchange.

Including market and adaptation information significantly improves the concept of interdependence. This is easily illustrated using a third state to represent possible market options. To show that interdependence often is absent even in high volumes of economic interaction and present in situations where direct trade is negligible, three hypothetical scenarios follow. The first scenario represents the traditional direct dyadic conceptualization of economic interdependence. The second scenario shows how two states can be engaged in a high level of trade, but market conditions are such that neither state faces high costs in the event that their economic relationship deteriorates. Finally, the third scenario shows how two states can experience interdependence without significant levels of trade with each other. This highlights the drawbacks of focusing only on trade and ignoring the indirect market effects.

Scenario 1: Current Interpretations of Economic Interdependence

Figure 2.1 displays three traditional conceptualizations of economic interdependence. In each case, there are two states, A and B. Case one represents a dyad that is characterized by what Barbieri would identify as salient and symmetric economic interdependence. While operationalizations vary across studies, all of these studies operationalize the economic relationships using some function of directional trade. In case one, this trade function exhibits a high level of dependence for both states upon each other. Case two also exhibits symmetry in the economic relationship between the dyad, but at a very low salience level, indicating two states that are economically independent from each other. Finally, case three shows a dyad that is characterized by salient but asymmetric economic interdependence, as only one of the states has a high degree of dependence while the other has a low or moderate degree of dependence.

All three cases in scenario one are dyadic. The interdependence between the two states is a function of their dyadic interaction. No information is given regarding the ability of either state to seek other trading partners. How do the states cope if their economic relationship is severed? The implicit assumption is that the welfare gains achieved from economic interaction are completely lost. Scenarios two and three below reveal how reliance on this dyadic perspective produces an incomplete picture.

Figure 2.1. The Traditional Economic Interdependence Argument

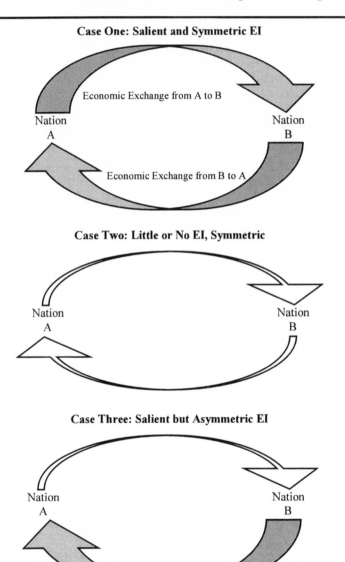

Case One: Salient and Symmetric EI

Economic Exchange from A to B

Nation A

Nation B

Economic Exchange from B to A

Case Two: Little or No EI, Symmetric

Nation A

Nation B

Case Three: Salient but Asymmetric EI

Nation A

Nation B

Scenario Two: Salient and Symmetric Trade without Interdependence

Scenario two (figure 2.2) provides an example of how we misinterpret trade activity as economic interdependence. State C represents the possible market options for A and B. For simplicity, assume that there are only three states in the market. State C can engage in economic ties with either A or B such that both A and B are able to substitute the good(s) they get from their original trading partner. This substitution is inefficient relative to the original relationship between A and B (assuming that A and B are maximizing efficiency and welfare), but still more efficient than autarky (no trade). Hirschman argues that this ability to import goods or export goods to a third party ameliorates the economic dependence of State A (B) on State B (A):

> A country menaced with an interruption of trade with a given country has the alternative of diverting its trade to a third country; by doing so it evades more or less completely the damaging consequences of the stoppage of its trade with one particular country. (1945: 29)

When opportunities to shift economic activity to another state in the marketplace are present, states A and B are interacting, *but they are not interdependent.* The exit option introduces fungibility into the economic relationship. Although this option may involve short-term costs to one or both states, the potential for new outlets for economic relations provides each nation with alternatives other than the absence of trade. These alternatives may become very important in the event of political or economic externalities that may disrupt or threaten to disrupt the flow of economic activity.

Placing the dyadic economic relationship between A and B within the context of the marketplace radically alters the concept of interdependence. It is not enough that states A and B have salient or intense trade ties. In order for interdependence to exist, they must also lack the exit option such that their only alternative to trading with one another is extremely costly or a return to the conditions of autarky. The key question is how costly it would be for A or B to shift its trade ties to C. Symmetry in interdependence is similarly refined. If only one state (A or B) enjoys the opportunity to exit to the market for its imports and exports, then asymmetric interdependence exists between the two states. In all cases, the added information of the nature of the marketplace is necessary to identify properly the existence and character of the AB dyad's economic interdependence.

Figure 2.2. Salient and Symmetric Trade, but No Interdependence

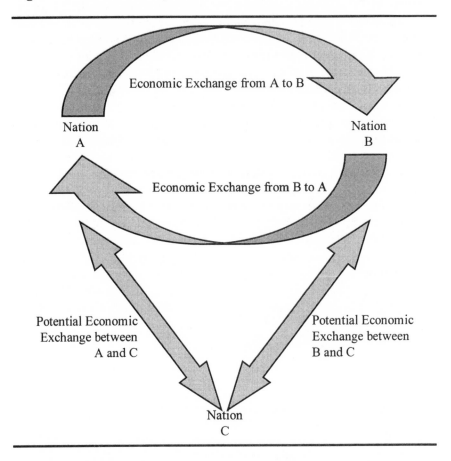

Scenario Three: Indirect Interdependence

Scenario three (figure 2.3) also introduces state C to represent the marketplace. In scenario two, the market did not have to play an active economic role with either of the other states to influence the AB dyad. In this scenario, assume that C is actively trading the same good with states

A and B. For example, state C may be importing oil from A and B in exchange for capital. Assume also that states A and B do not have a direct trading relationship that one would consider to be salient or intense. Despite having no direct economic activity, the AB dyad may be economically interdependent. In this case, A and B are interdependent with respect to the price level of the good they are both exchanging with the market. Either state can change the economic relationship between its dyadic competitor and the third party. For example, if B opts to reduce its price of oil exports to C, A must also reduce its price of oil or face changes in its trading relationship with C.[6] This can lead to a transformation from case one to case two in figure 2.3. Case one illustrates the scenario with A and B trading similar goods with the market (C), but not each other. Case two illustrates the potential damage that B can do to A's trading activity by undercutting A's price levels and garnering a larger share of the market activity.

Using the previous conceptualizations we would not characterize the AB dyad as economically interdependent. By adding the context of the marketplace, however, we see that in this case A and B are interdependent. Continuing with the example of oil, the loss in capital that would be incurred by A by a drop in oil prices by B could have serious domestic repercussions. If we assume the market to have a fixed (or at least inelastic) total demand for oil, then State A cannot fully recover from this loss unless State B reverts its oil prices back to the original level. This demonstrates an economic interdependence between states A and B that could not be observed empirically by a purely dyadic operationalization of interdependence focusing on trade.

To illustrate this scenario, consider the precrisis events surrounding Iraq's invasion of Kuwait in the fall of 1990. Years of war between Iraq and Iran depleted Iraq's oil export production, which hindered the country's ability to repay its loans to Kuwait and other Arab states. After failed attempts to get its debts cancelled, Iraq began in the summer of 1990 to protest Kuwait's oil exporting practices. On May 28, 1990, Saddam Hussein claimed that Kuwait was purposefully overproducing oil. This overproduction led to a decrease in the world price for oil, furthering Iraq's inability to generate capital to repay its loans. Iraq soon added the charge that Kuwait was stealing oil from a disputed oil field. In short, Hussein accused Kuwait of dumping oil on the market and stealing the

Figure 2.3 Economic Interdependence with No Direct Trade

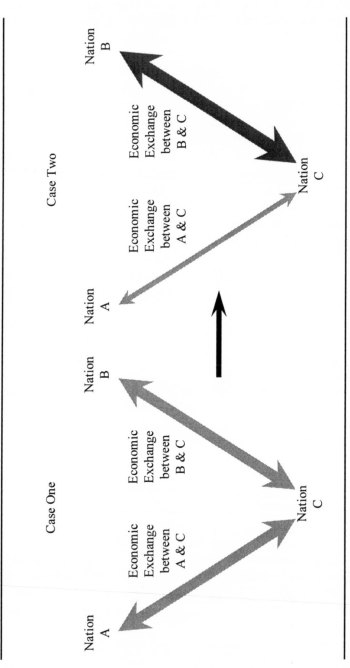

Case One: Nations A and B trade similar goods with Nation C, but not with each other.
Case Two: Nation B drops its prices for exports to C, causing C to import more from B and less from A.

necessary supply of oil to maintain such a practice. Negotiations were short-lived, and in August the Iraqi forces invaded Kuwait (Brecher and Wilkenfeld, 1997).

A territorial dispute over the Bubiyan and Warba islands accounts for much of the enduring tension between these two states, but in 1990 it was their economic interdependence that provided the spark of military conflict. Despite dyadic trade levels that accounted for less than 3 percent of each state's total trade, Iraq was dependent upon Kuwait and the other oil exporting states to maintain a world oil price level that would allow Iraq to repay its debts and rebuild its armed forces.[7] Kuwait's increased oil production drove down the cost of oil in the world market, making Iraq's oil exports less profitable. In this illustration, Kuwait's market power combined with Iraq's domestic dependence on oil for revenue to create a high level of interdependence. This interdependence was asymmetrical, as Iraq's debts made it more vulnerable than Kuwait to the effects of a change in oil prices.

Defining Economic Interdependence: A Return to Exit Costs

> Large volumes of trade between or among prospective belligerents, however, are not necessarily a valid indicator of trade-related opportunity costs of war. Instead, what really matters is whether close substitutes exist for the export markets and imports that prewar trading partners supplied. (Joanne Gowa, 1994: 118)

The three scenarios demonstrate two points. First, economic interdependence is not merely a function of current economic activity. It is a function of economic activity within the context of the alternatives available to both states. If we assume that states are involved in economic relationships that maximize welfare, then the costs involved in exiting these relationships are essentially what is lost in switching from this "best" option to the next best alternative. These alternatives could involve other trading partners or a return to autarky (economic isolation), where all the goods and services previously obtained from a trading partner must be substituted with domestic alternatives. I define the opportunity costs associated with these alternatives as *exit costs*. Exit costs occur only when states exit an economic relationship with one another. Exit costs are analogous to Baldwin's use of the term opportunity costs, but I adopt the new terminology to highlight economic exit as the source of the opportunity costs.

Thus, it is not enough to characterize economic interdependence by the existing economic ties between states. We must also know how costly it will be to both states if these ties are broken. Therefore, we need to identify the conditions which lead to exit costs. These conditions are asset specificity and market structure, and are addressed in turn below.

Asset Specificity

The literature on transaction cost economics, the foundation of which is provided by Oliver Williamson (1975; 1985; 1996), sheds considerable light on the factors that drive up the costs of exit. This literature keys on adaptation as the central problem of organization. Change in real-world economic factors is ever present (i.e., new oil fields are discovered, or the implementation of nuclear power decreases the demand for oil), and economic actors must try to organize their relations with respect to the potential hazards that accompany their transactions.

Transaction costs can occur on two levels. There are always accepted costs that are a part of the normal interaction between two states. Establishing economic links between states is not cost free. For example, trade routes require the capacity to transport goods and services across geographical and political boundaries. The economic infrastructure between states is often complex and expensive, and states willingly bear these costs in order to attain the benefits that motivate the economic ties (assuming, of course, that the benefits here outweigh these costs). These costs are sunk costs, made by a state in order to enjoy the benefits of trade. There exists, however, the potential for unexpected costs as a result of changes in the relationship or the economic infrastructure between those states. These are the costs associated with adaptation.

The key element to understanding the extent of the costs of adaptation lies in the specificity of the assets involved in the establishment and continuation of the existing economic transaction. Williamson discusses asset specificity and the potential hazards that accompany it:

> Asset specificity has reference to the degree to which an asset can be redeployed to alternative uses and by alternative users without sacrifice of productive value. This has a relation to the notion of sunk cost. (1996: 59)

Continuing with the example of oil, consider the oil shock imposed by OPEC in the early 1970s as an illustration of the importance of asset specificity. Countries such as the United States faced steep adaptation costs in the face of the sharp decline in oil supply. Assets, such as capital and labor, were diverted to the internal production of oil and alternate energy sources. New domestic sources of oil were tapped by mining the relatively inefficient oil fields in Texas, Alaska, and California. At the same time, the United States developed its nuclear, solar, water, and even wind sources of energy. Diesel fuel consumption increased dramatically. Existing technology and investments, however, hindered these efforts. Factories and vehicles relied on oil products, and even as technologies for alternate energy became more readily available, refitting factories and replacing the fleet of cars and trucks proved to be far too costly. The costs of adaptation for the United States were enormous not only because of the volume of oil that was previously being consumed, but also because of the huge costs associated with replacing the assets that were specifically designed to process the oil into energy.

Another example of assets that are highly specific can be found in the aircraft manufacturing industry. As the largest aircraft manufacturer in the world, Boeing had invested billions of U.S. dollars to create the infrastructure needed to build airplanes. In addition, it employs tens of thousands of people. This capital and labor has been specifically invested toward the production of aircraft. As long as the demand for Boeing's product is strong, this investment is ideal. Commercial aircraft are remarkably expensive, however, and their operation costs are among other things a function of the fuel they consume. In times of economic contraction, governments and airline companies who are largely responsible for purchasing these planes cut back on their demand.

The problem for Boeing and its employees is that the demand for their planes is more elastic than Boeing's capacity to supply a product. The factory infrastructure that cost billions of dollars to produce cannot be easily adapted to manufacture other goods (such as cars or boats) in the event of a drop in demand. When the demand for new planes goes down, Boeing cuts production, incurs a loss in revenue, and lays off thousands of its employees. These costs are so intense precisely because the capital and labor assets that go into the operation of building planes are not fungible.

Not all assets are so specific. The Archer, Daniels, Midland (ADM) corporation is a pioneer in the production of soybean products. They have diversified the production of soybeans into a myriad of products ranging from tofu (a bean curd food product) to animal feed for livestock. ADM's ability to adapt the basic product of the soybean into multiple final products makes the assets which go into soybean production less specific with respect to any one of these final products. This allows

ADM to shift its assets involved in turning soybeans into consumable products to reflect changes in consumer markets. In turn, ADM is less dependent on any one market for its goods, reducing the exit costs it would face in the event that demand for a product such as tofu diminishes.

Hirschman also recognizes the importance of asset specificity in determining exit costs. Using the term "mobility of resources" Hirschman details how the fungibility of assets can divert exit costs. This mobility of resources includes

> the possibility of diverting capital goods to new purposes (i.e., their more or less "specific" character), the geographical mobility of the factors of production, and, above all, the ability of labor to turn to new tasks. (1945: 28)

Resources that are rigid in their relation to an international economic relationship make states vulnerable to their trading partners. Resources that are more mobile or fungible enable states to adapt to potential changes that other states may threaten to impose.

Market Structure

Asset specificity refers to the ability of states to adapt their factors of production in the event that they experience a shift in supply and demand in the international market. Market structure, on the other hand, determines the extent to which economic exit by a trading partner will generate the need to alter these factors of production. Scenarios two and three above demonstrate how market structure dictates a state's ability to find new markets for its imports and exports. A state that incurs economic exit from a trading partner may have other potential partners with which to establish new ties. As these alternate trading partners become scarce, current relationships become more costly to break. Gowa identifies this ability to find substitutes in the market as the key to opportunity costs:

> If such substitutes exist, then the trade-related opportunity costs of war will be low. This is precisely what the dispersion of market power implies: the existence of substitutes for import and export markets (1994: 118).

A market structure that provides easily accessible substitutes will ameliorate any potential costs of economic exit from trading partners.

The market power generated by OPEC in the 1970s is critical to understanding why the United States scrambled to find alternatives to oil. OPEC's successful cartel behavior eliminated competition between the Middle East oil exporting states. This lack of competition led to monopolistic power for the OPEC countries. When acting together, they were able to set supply levels and oil prices arbitrarily. While asset specificity explains why the United States was forced to pay higher oil prices, market structure explains why the United States could not turn to other countries for its oil needs.

Just as the lack of competition in suppliers of goods results in monopoly power, a dearth of consumers can also lead to monopsony power. The United States is often considered to have monopsony power in that it is the largest single consumer market in the world. Its sheer size and purchasing power enables it to alter world price levels and shape economic interaction in ways that would not be possible if it were a smaller consumer market (Krugman and Obstfeld, 1991). China's future market is frequently touted as the great consumer market of the twenty-first century. Even the anticipation of this monopsony power has empowered China to shape its international economic relations.

Together, market power interacts with asset specificity to delineate the context within which economic interaction takes place. Embedding dyadic economic activity within this systemic and domestic context provides more accurate and complex information about the economic relationship. We are now ready to define economic interdependence as a function of exit costs:

Definition: *Economic Interdependence* exists when there are exit costs for any two states vis-à-vis their economic relationship. These costs are a function of market structure, asset specificity, and salience. The salience of interaction exacerbates interdependence, but only when market conditions constrain adaptation. Thus, the highest forms of interdependence exist when exit options are scarce, adaptation is costly, and the economic relationship is highly salient.

Market structure and asset specificity are the building blocks of exit costs. Qualifications between sensitivity and vulnerability become unnecessary at this point, although of the two concepts this definition falls squarely in the vulnerability camp (Baldwin, 1980). The added depth with respect to the source of exit costs makes it unique from any previous definition. With the concept of economic interdependence explicitly defined and properly segregated from other forms of economic activity, the next section provides a conceptual definition of political conflict.

Political Conflict: Violent and Nonviolent Conflict

The final task of this chapter is to specify the concept of political conflict. Conflict is more easily observed than economic interdependence,
and the study of conflict has been extensive. The scientific study of war
dates back to the early twentieth century and Lewis Fry Richardson
(1960). Seminal works by Wright (1965) and Singer and Small (1972),
as well as more recent contributions (Vasquez, 1993), have definitively
set forth rigorous concepts of war. Others have expanded their attention
from war to international crises and militarized disputes that may or may
not escalate to war (Snyder and Diesing, 1977; Jones et al., 1996; Brecher and Wilkenfeld, 1997). As such, the task at hand here is one of iden-
tification rather than development. In the literature reviewed above, political conflict typically takes the form of interstate war or militarized
interstate disputes. Polachek (1980) adopts a broader concept of conflict,
arguing that interdependence influences political behavior at lower levels
of conflict as well as extreme events such as war.

    This study differs from previous investigations of interdependence
and conflict in that I disaggregate the presence of conflict into two categories: low- and high-level conflict. The motivation for this lies in Keohane and Nye's claim that interdependence provides states with an alternative to violence in dispute resolution. Two states that are economically
interdependent can link their economic and political behavior. The economic relationship becomes an alternate and more efficient arena for dispute resolution, thereby reducing the need for more traditional tools of
conflict such as military force. This perspective differs greatly from the
idea that interdependence fosters cooperation and a utopian world.
Rather, states are able to use the more efficient (less costly) arena of
power generated by economic interdependence to resolve their differences. The interaction is still conflictual, but the battlefield is an economic rather than a military one. This is not to say that the option of
higher levels of conflict is removed for states, only that in some circumstances the use of lower levels of conflict may be the most effective option.[8] The chapters below will seek to identify this link between economic interdependence and lower levels of conflict, if it exists. Thus, I
employ the following conceptual definitions to cover the range of political behavior pertinent to this study:

Definition: *Low-level conflict* includes the use of diplomatic and economic tools by one state in an attempt to persuade or coerce another
state.

High-level conflict includes the use of military tools by one state in an attempt to persuade or coerce another state. The absence of either type of conflict is construed as peace. This includes cooperation as well as neutral interaction.

The result is a hierarchical scale of political conflict. The occurrence of high-level conflict assumes that low-level conflict has also occurred.

I assume throughout this book that when conflict occurs between two states it is motivated by some disagreement over an issue or set of issues. This spark of conflict, however, is not necessarily related to economic interdependence. Conflict need not be motivated by economic interdependence to qualify for consideration in this study. The approach taken here is to investigate whether economic interdependence has an impact on conflict that is motivated by *any* issue.[9]

Conclusion

The review of the literature in chapter 1 on the economic interdependence-political conflict puzzle suggests that the concept of economic interdependence has been underspecified. As a result, the term "interdependence" has been interchanged with terms like trade, interaction, and integration. This murkiness, combined with the rather oppressive agendas of the various liberalist and realist camps, has inhibited our ability to grasp the causal mechanisms by which interdependence and conflict may be linked. By reintroducing the notion that interdependence is a product of exit costs, and by detailing the structural factors which generate these costs, I have addressed the conceptual gaps in the literature regarding economic interdependence.

Having established definitions of economic interdependence and political conflict, the next step is to develop a causal theory that explicates if, when, and how the two phenomena may be linked. Chapter 3 begins this task with a discussion of the use of economic tools in political bargaining, and then develops a strategic model that captures the role of economic interdependence in the initiation and escalation of interstate conflict.

Notes

1. Just how high is "high enough" is a question that will be tackled in chapter 3.
2. See Baldwin (1980) and Cooper (1985) for a historical perspective on the conceptual evolution of economic interdependence.
3. The association of these terms with interdependence is often credited to Keohane and Nye, but their use to discuss interdependence appears in an earlier article by Kenneth Waltz (1970).
4. As we will see below, because each state's dependence is a function of the sum of exports and imports between the two, if this aggregation of trade is nonzero for one state in a dyad, it is also nonzero for the other state. Thus, it is impossible for one state to be totally nondependent on another state unless the same is true in reverse.
5. In response, Barbieri also calculates the *TradeShare* scores using GDP instead of total trade.
6. This, of course, assumes that state B has the capacity to increase its supply of oil to state C to compensate for the added demand generated by lower prices.
7. Source for trade data is Barbieri (2002). Trade between Iraq and Kuwait was at or below 3 percent of the total trade for each state in the five years before the conflict. Mean scores from 1963-1990 are less than 2 percent for both states.
8. Chapter 3 is concerned with exactly when this low-level conflict option is optimal for states.
9. In chapter 3, I discuss the special case of when the motivating issue driving conflict is economic in nature.

3

Solving the Puzzle:
A Model of Economic Interdependence
and Political Conflict

The conceptual development in chapter 2 sets the stage for a discussion on the linkage between economic interdependence and political conflict. Adding the dimensions of market structure and asset specificity shifts the focus within economic interdependence from trade volumes to exit costs. Broadening the scope of political conflict allows us to consider non-violent as well as violent forms of conflict. With these concepts in place, this chapter returns to the questions of whether and how economic interdependence and political conflict are linked. Does economic interdependence reduce conflict as states become constrained politically by their pursuit of welfare? Does this interdependence provide one more source of conflict, as uneven gains in wealth drive states further apart? Is this linkage real or imagined?

Chapter 1 cites recent empirical research providing affirmative answers to all three of these questions (Kim, 1995; Barbieri, 1996; Oneal and Russett, 1997). Either the linkage between these two phenomena is unstable or it is more complex than current theory suggests. Before continuing our search for empirical solutions to this puzzle, an examination of the theory underlying this causal linkage may help us to re-specify the empirical analysis. In turn, this may help to sort out the evidence at hand. This theoretical examination is the task of this chapter. The next section introduces the notion of interdependence as a source of bargaining power. I then extend this bargaining power logic to address the linkage between interdependence and conflict. I develop a theory of the relationship between economic interdependence and political conflict using this bargaining power approach. Analysis of the theoretical model indicates that all three relationships (interdependence leads to peace, leads to conflict, or has no impact) are possible. Only by considering the costs of economic exit along with the parameters surrounding interstate disputes can we ascertain when to expect each form of linkage to occur.

Interdependence and Bargaining

The focus on trade as an incentive or disincentive for conflict has dominated the study of the trade-conflict puzzle, but several studies have identified flaws in this logic. Baldwin (1985) emphasizes that when states practice economic statecraft—the use of economics as a political tool—they consider the potential losses they face from trade loss within the context of other policy alternatives. It is not enough to point out that loss of trade associated with conflict is costly. Rather, one must study how states evaluate these costs relative to the costs and benefits associated with other policy options. For example, the costs of losing wealth associated with trade may be minor when stacked up against the costs of meeting the demands of another country. In short, the *ceteris paribus* assumptions that facilitate the linear relationship between trade and conflict may be inappropriate.

Baldwin's (1985) study of economic statecraft emphasizes the use of economic ties as an effective policy tool that is an *alternative* to traditional military conflict. Keohane and Nye (1989) key in on the manipulation of economic interdependence as an alternative to military means. While they do not claim that military power has passed its prime as the ultimate political tool, they do argue "there is no guarantee that military means will be more effective than economic ones to achieve a given purpose" (17). This path leads to a research question that is fundamentally different from the search for the existence and direction of a basic relationship between economics and conflict. The question instead becomes: can the economic relations between two states generate the ability of one state to influence the other *without* resorting to military means, thereby reducing violent conflict? In other words, can the economic ties create bargaining power? If so, then the idea that trade weaves a web of peace and prosperity no longer necessarily holds. Instead, economic ties generate an added realm within which world politics can operate.

The notion that economic influence provides an effective alternative to the military option is rooted in the argument that asymmetry in an economic relationship generates asymmetry in power. For any given pair of states, both gain from trading with one another but one state is typically more dependent than the other (unless they are exactly equal in their dependence). This relative difference within the interdependence is what drives political opportunity. Instead of generating violent conflict between states, however, this asymmetry provides the opportunity for these states to use relative economic power as leverage in political bargaining. The resulting political interaction is still conflictual, but the arena for conflict is economic rather than military. Developed first by Hirschman and adopted later by Keohane and Nye, this notion of bargaining power remains one of the few theoretical alternatives to the monotonic relationships discussed in chapter 1.

The Bargaining Approach

Over half a century has passed since Albert Hirschman wrote *National Power and the Structure of Foreign Trade* (1945), yet it remains the most persuasive argument in favor of the importance of political influence generated by an economic relationship. He points out that the mere potential for interrupting trade can lead to power:

> Tariff wars and interruptions of trade rarely occur, but the awareness of their possibility is sufficient to test the influence of the stronger country and to shape the policy of the weaker. (1945: 16)

The potential for trade interruption creates an opportunity for the state that is best suited to cope with the trade loss. Hirschman then links this economic power with the ability to exert political influence:

> The power to interrupt commercial or financial relations with any country . . . is the root cause of the influence or power position which a country acquires in other countries. (16)

Unfortunately, Hirschman does not get more explicit when discussing this linkage, and the primary focus of his book rests on how a state acquires this power to manipulate others. This leaves the reader to complete the argument that when one state has this economic power over another state, it somehow translates this power into political influence.

Decades later, Keohane and Nye echoed Hirschman's analysis that asymmetry can generate political bargaining power. They argue that asymmetrical economic interdependence provides a political resource to the less dependent state. This state can effectively threaten to make changes in its economic relationships with more dependent states to bring about political change (1989: 11). Similarly to Hirschman, however, Keohane and Nye do not specify the mechanism by which states link their relative economic power to a favorable political outcome. They simply postulate that asymmetry in interdependence provides bargaining power in politics.

Not all scholars have been supportive of the idea that economic ties can generate political influence. The critique set forth by Wagner calls into question this notion of bargaining power from economic interdependence (1988). The basic thrust of this critique is that while the arguments of Hirschman and Keohane and Nye seem highly intuitive, they suffer from several key flaws. Wagner points out that Hirschman's arguments suffer from what Harsanyi labeled "the Blackmailer's Fallacy." This fallacy is the belief that if a nation (nation B) would rather give in to a demand by another nation (nation A) than suffer some form of punishment, then it is possible for nation A to successfully extract this demand by merely threatening nation B with the punishment.[1] Wagner argues:

> Such reasoning ignores the importance of the value that A assigns to the [demand] in question, as well as the cost to A of executing the threat. (1988: 474)

In essence, the danger here is in ignoring the possibility that nation A has made a threat that it cannot enforce. If the threatened punishment is more costly to nation A than foregoing its demand, then nation A may find itself unable to follow through on the threat. Baldwin (1985) also recognizes the need to assess the relative costs and benefits associated with the demand and the threat for each actor. It is crucial to be able to compare the value of the demand for each with the cost of executing or enduring the consequences of the threat associated with the demand.

Wagner's strongest criticism, however, is reserved for Keohane and Nye's argument that it is the asymmetry in interdependence that generates bargaining power. He formalizes this argument by employing various adaptations of the Nash bargaining game (where players, or in this case nations, seek to divide a pile of money). He captures asymmetry in interdependence by making the discount rates unequal for the two countries. That is, one country is better equipped than the other to delay agreement until it receives the distribution of money that it wants. The less dependent state, therefore, can be more patient than its bargaining partner. Wagner then introduces a political dimension by allowing the less dependent state to demand that the other state yield on some political issue. He finds, however, that attaching such a political demand only serves to reduce the less dependent state's share of the pile of money which is being bargained over. The less dependent state must compensate the more dependent state for the political concession. Based on this analysis, he concludes:

> If "asymmetrical interdependence" means that one party to a mutually beneficial economic relationship needs the benefits from it more than another, then asymmetrical economic interdependence does not imply that the less dependent actor will be able to exercise political influence over the other. (1988: 481)

Any successful link between economic interdependence and political influence has to make both states better off than if they had bargained over the economic dimension alone. Further, this result has nothing to do with the asymmetry in the economic ties.

Wagner has encountered little response to his critique. Keohane and Nye concede that asymmetries do not provide necessary or sufficient conditions for bargaining power (Keohane and Nye, 1989: 252), although they do not interpret his critique as derailing their general approach. I am less willing to close the door on this debate, however, especially with respect to the idea of economic interdependence as a substitute bargaining currency to the military alternative. Wagner's conclusions are a function of the game he chooses to represent the bargaining situation. While the Nash bargaining model is a natural first choice, before we rely on the analysis of any model it behooves us to assess how well it captures the essence of the story we wish to tell.

Wagner bases his analysis on a story where two players of unequal strength and wealth are negotiating over how to split a fixed pile of money. In the event that the players cannot come to an agreement over the distribution of the money, both sides walk away with nothing. In this story, evaluating asymmetry and bargaining power depends on how the division of this money can be influenced by the less dependent player. At the heart of the Keohane and Nye argument, however, is the idea that economic tools are substitutable for military ones. The political issue is not a rider attached to the negotiations over the distribution of cash, but rather *it is the primary subject of negotiation*. More importantly, if the two players cannot come to an agreement over how to distribute the pile of money, or whatever issue they are bargaining over, then they will consider fighting over it instead of walking away.

If this is the case, then perhaps the bargaining model employed by Wagner is inappropriate. What Wagner perhaps does not fully consider is the options facing these nations if they fail to resolve their dispute using economic leverage. If an economic relationship is exploited by one state to influence another over an issue or dispute that may alternatively be addressed in the military arena, then the costs and benefits of this military alternative need to be considered. Not reaching a bargaining agreement may lead states to forfeit the pile of money or issue the states are bargaining over; but it can also lead to a fight.

If two states are negotiating over an issue that may be the subject of a potential miltary dispute, then the specter of the military option should enter their decision calculations. If bargaining with economic interdependence works the way Keohane and Nye suggest, then it serves as a proxy battlefield, more efficient and far less costly than its military alternative. Economic costs are not the only potential costs to be considered here. Nations weigh these exit costs against the alternatives: leaving the dispute unresolved, or resolving the dispute via military means. This cost-benefit analysis is more complex than the basic cost-benefit analysis discussed above. Its complexity highlights the need for theory that explicates the causal linkage between economic interdependence and political conflict.

In the next section, I present an alternative to the bargaining model used by Wagner. I agree that the only way to establish definitively the utility (or lack thereof) of economic interdependence as a political tool is through the development of more explicit theory. The informal arguments set forth by Hirschman and Keohane and Nye are intuitive, but in the end are unable to stand up to Wagner's analysis. This is because both Hirschman and Keohane and Nye suggest that economic interdependence affects politics but never elaborate how this linkage occurs. Wagner's formalization of this linkage is important in that it demonstrates the need for an explicit theory, but in the end it overlooks the role of high-level conflict and the political issues at stake.

A Model of Bargaining, Threat, and Economic Exit

It may be useful to begin the modeling process with a simple story reflecting the logic of the theory developed below. For this example, I turn to that most sophisticated arena of bargaining and strategy: lunchtime at a typical elementary school. One day, two young schoolchildren (let us call them Chris and Terry), are standing in line in the school cafeteria.

Chris and Terry are lab partners in science class. As such, they work as a team in class, which saves time and improves their grades. They are not required to be lab partners, as all of the students in the science class have the option of doing the work by themselves. Nevertheless, it is a good partnership, something that both students value.

As they are standing in line in the cafeteria, Chris realizes that he is very hungry but has no money to buy his lunch. His requests for a loan from the students around him fall on deaf ears, and it becomes apparent that if he wants to eat lunch he will have to persuade someone else to give up his or her lunch money. A rather dubious solution to his dilemma pops into his head: perhaps he can use his lab partnership with Terry as leverage to get his lunch money. That is, if he threatens to terminate their lab partnership unless Terry turns over the money, Terry may give in to his demand. Chris knows that Terry will not be very amenable to the idea, as Terry needs his money to buy his own lunch.

Chris can think of two ways to try to persuade Terry to give up his money. First, he can threaten to break up the lab partnership. If that strategy fails, his second and more severe strategy is to threaten to fight Terry for the money. Chris knows Terry may not respond to the threats. Losing the lab partnership and getting into a fight are real possibilities. Before Chris decides whether to demand Terry's lunch money, he has to think things through.

First, Chris must determine if he is willing to end the lab partnership if Terry does not give him the lunch money. What happens if Terry refuses his demand? Chris could back down and withdraw his threat, but then he would lose face in front of the other students in line. If Chris follows through with his threat, he will terminate the lab partnership. This is unappealing to both students, as they will have to find other partners or do the lab work by themselves. Breaking up the lab partnership, however, is more costly for Terry than it is for Chris. Let us assume that Mary, who is also in the science class, is looking for a lab partner and would like to study with Chris but not with Terry. To make matters worse, Terry is struggling in the science class, and the thought of going it alone in the lab makes Terry very nervous. Both students are aware that Chris and Mary could easily be lab partners while Terry would have to work on his own.

Chris also considers what he will do next if Terry will not give up the money and Chris exits the lab partnership. Chris will still need the money, and with the lab partnership defunct, the only available option would be to threaten a fight or give up. If Chris threatens a fight, Terry would have another chance to give up the money. If he still refuses to give Chris the money, however, the two will fight for it. This outcome is costly for both boys as well, and they hope to avoid fighting if possible. Neither student knows who will win the fight, but they both will end up with cuts, scrapes, and bruises. Although fighting is not an ideal outcome, Chris considers the ramifications of the fight before deciding whether to make the initial demand.

Now consider the situation from Terry's point of view. In the event that Chris does demand the money from Terry, threatening him with ending the lab partnership if he does not comply, Terry will have some quick thinking to do. First, he will determine whether keeping the money is worth risking the lab partnership. Giving up the money means going hungry, but losing the lab partnership means working alone in science class. Second, he must consider whether Chris really will end the partnership if Terry refuses to give up the money. If Chris is bluffing, then Terry is better off by not giving in. Finally, if things really go wrong, he needs to assess his own ability to win the fight.

Both students consider the alternative outcomes they may face. They know each other well, and each student knows the other's strategy. They also know how much each student values the lunch money and the lab partnership. They know it would be embarrassing to Chris if he makes a threat and then fails to follow through, and they know what is at stake if they decide to fight. The only thing the students do not know with certainty is who will win the fight if it occurs.

Figure 3.1 summarizes this scenario. How can one predict what each student will do in this situation? The key for both students is the cost-benefit analysis they face as they compare the possible outcomes. Terry cannot afford to lose Chris as a lab partner over his lunch money, and they both know it. Having weighed his decision carefully and considering all of the possible outcomes, Chris demands the lunch money from Terry, threatening the lab partnership if Terry does not give in. Terry has little choice but to comply.

This story reflects the basic logic of the model I will develop below. Chris wants something that Terry has, and he considers the threat of exit as a means to getting the lunch money. Both boys must consider their options within the dimensions of the game. They assess the immediate choices they face, the availability of new lab partners, and their abilities to go it alone in the lab in the event that their lab partnership comes to an end. The crowded lunchroom adds the dimension of an audience that alters the willingness of each child to give in or back down. Finally, the risk of conflict hangs over their interactions.

There are many ways to expand, alter, or add to this story. For example, Terry could counteroffer with an offer to split the money, or Chris could demand some of Terry's money so that both students can eat something. Mary could enter the game as a third player. We could relax the assumption that Chris and Terry both know how much the other wants to eat lunch or wants to stay partners. Elementary school life can get quite complicated, and the same is certainly true about world politics. It is useful, however, to map this basic story to a formal model and see what leverage it provides in the interdependence-conflict puzzle.

It is important to note that this story is different from the model used by Wagner or the story told by Angell (chapter 2). In Wagner's model the two children would be bargaining over the amount of effort each student would put into the lab partnership. Chris has the option of linking Terry's lunch money to the negotiations. Angell's story would focus on only the lab partnership, where Chris would threaten to exit the relationship if Terry does not do more work.

The model presented below is not the only type of linkage between interdependence and conflict. It does, however, develop the existence and character of a causal link between these two phenomena.

Figure 3.1. Lab Partnerships and Lunch Money

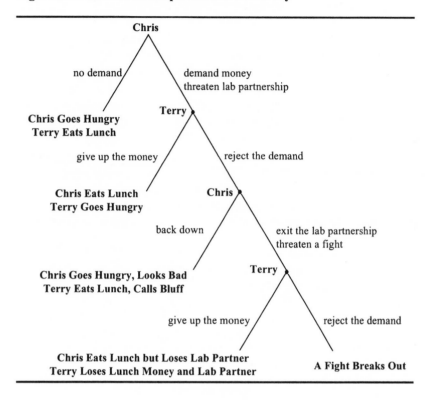

Lunch Money and Lab Partnerships in World Politics

Can this story involving two elementary schoolchildren be applied to the interaction between two nations? Hirschman indicates that the use of an interstate economic relationship can be used in much the same way that Chris can use the lab partnership:

> [E]conomic pressure upon a country consists mainly of the threat of severance and ultimately of actual interruption of external economic relations . . . (1945: 16)

This economic pressure serves as leverage in one state's attempt to exert power over another. The threat can be a threat of economic sanctions or a threat to take one's business elsewhere, but it involves economic exit in some fashion. This ability to use the economic interdependence between the two states as a political bargaining tool is a function of the exit costs faced by each state. Chapter 2 demonstrated that market structure and adaptation drive these exit costs. Now we are ready to embed these exit costs in the context of the bargaining process to see if, when, and how economic interdependence can generate political power. Below I develop the model of this bargaining-threat interaction in world politics. Game theory is used to highlight the strategic manipulation of economic interdependence. While there are significant drawbacks to the game-theoretic approach, it provides an intuitive platform from which to explore the way states link conflict and economics.[2]

There are two states in the model: a Challenger and a Target. The Challenger wants something from the Target, and it must decide whether to demand it or forego any effort to obtain what it desires. For example, the Challenger may wish to reclaim territory, as was the case in 1982 when Great Britain demanded that Argentina relinquish its claim on the South Georgia and South Sandwich Islands. This demand can also be strictly political, as in a call for change in another country's human rights policy. It can even be an economic demand, as in Iceland's demand to extend its exclusive fishing rights to fifty miles from its coast, at the expense of British and West German access.

The Target, on the other hand, desires the status quo. The Challenger must decide whether to use its economic ties with the Target to help extract its demand. To do this, the Challenger attaches the threat of economic exit to the demand. This game structure captures the reactive demand behavior of international economic sanctions as well as the proactive behavior by the Challenger when it seeks to revise the status quo.

If the Challenger issues the demand, using the threat of economic exit as leverage, the Target decides whether to comply with the demand or stand firm and incur the exit costs. If the Target rejects the demand, the Challenger may choose to exit the economic relationship and renew its demand. With the economic ties severed, the only leverage remaining for the Challenger is to threaten the use of military force unless the Target complies. If the Target still refuses the Challenger's demands, the use of economic tools to resolve the dispute has failed and the players escalate to the arena of military force. This game reflects Keohane and Nye's argument that states use economic tools in bargaining without sacrificing the opportunity to use military tools if necessary. It will also allow us to ask if and when economic interdependence can prove effective in bargaining, thereby replacing military force as the tool of choice when resolving disputes. The details of this game structure follow, along with a formal analysis of the model.

The Game

The Challenger makes the first move, and it faces the choice of whether to make a political demand upon the Target or remain at the status quo. This demand is accompanied by a threat of economic exit by the Challenger. The Target makes the second move of this game: it can either comply with or reject the Challenger's demand. If the Target complies, the game ends with the Challenger gaining the utility of its demand, v_{Ch}, and the Target losing v_T.

If the Target rejects the initial demand, the game continues with the Challenger's second move. The Challenger can either make good on its threat of economic exit or back down, withdrawing its demand. Exiting the economic relationship does not relinquish the demand, however. Instead, the Challenger attaches the threat of military force to this demand, and prepares to shift the bargaining arena from economic to military dimensions. If the Challenger does not exit the economic relationship, the game ends with the Target calling its bluff. This brings with it audience costs, r_{Ch}, for the Challenger, and rewards, r_T, for the Target (Fearon, 1994). These audience costs can be domestic or international. Being caught bluffing reveals a certain incompetence in the leader's foreign policy skills (Smith, 1996) to domestic constituencies. At the international level, bluffing can lead other states not to take the Challenger seriously in the future. On the other hand, the Target enjoys the rewards that come with successfully standing up to the Challenger's demands. This enhances the Target's stature both at home and abroad.

If the Challenger elects to act on its threat and exit the relationship, the Target makes its final move of the game. Again, it chooses between rejecting and accepting the Challenger's demand. If the Target complies, the game ends with the Challenger gaining the value of its demand, v_{CH}, minus the costs that it incurs in the process of economic exit, e_{Ch}. The Target not only loses its value of the demand, v_T, but also the costs it endures from economic exit, e_T. If the Target rejects the demand, then the use of the economic threat to gain political demands has failed, and the states escalate to the use of high-level conflict (i.e., militarized conflict).

For simplicity, I represent the outcome of this escalated conflict as a lottery. This simplification focuses the analysis on how two states get involved in conflict. The Challenger wins the escalated conflict with probability p and loses with probability $1-p$. Win or lose, both states must pay the costs of economic exit, as well as a new set of costs associated with the high-level conflict, c_{Ch} and c_T. Rejecting the political demand a second time, then, produces the following expected utilities:

$$E(U_{Ch}|\text{Fight}) = p(v_{Ch} - e_{Ch} - c_{Ch}) + (1-p)(-e_{Ch} - c_{Ch}) \qquad (3.1)$$

$$E(U_T|\text{Fight}) = p(-v_T - e_T - c_T) + (1-p)(-e_T - c_T). \qquad (3.2)$$

Winning the conflict generates gains v_{Ch} for the Challenger, less the cost of economic exit and the cost of the conflict. If the Challenger loses, then the Target gets the benefit of remaining at the status quo minus the cost of enduring economic exit and the cost of conflict. Table 3.1 summarizes the expected utilities each state faces with respect to each potential outcome of the game. Figure 3.2 graphically depicts the game sequence.

Table 3.1. Expected Utilities

Challenger Move(s)	Target Move(s)	Outcome	Challenger's Expected Utility	Target's Expected Utility
No Demand		Status Quo	0	0
Demand	Comply	Challenger Compels Target w/ Threat	v_{Ch}	$-v_T$
Demand, No Exit	Reject	Challenger Backs Down	$-r_{Ch}$	r_T
Demand, Exit	Reject, Comply	Challenger Compels Target w/ Exit	$v_{Ch} - e_{Ch}$	$-v_T - e_T$
Demand, Exit	Reject, Reject	Escalated Political Conflict	$p(W_{Ch}) + (1-p)(L_{Ch})$ $=$ $p(v_{Ch} - e_{Ch} - c_{Ch})$ $+ (1-p)(-e_{Ch} - c_{Ch})$	$p(L_T) + (1-p)(W_T)$ $=$ $p(-v_T - e_T - c_T)$ $+ (1-p)(-e_T - c_T)$

Figure 3.2. A Bargaining Game

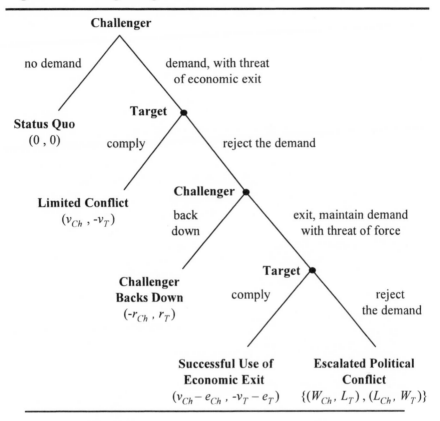

Challenger	Target
v_{Ch} = Value of Demand	v_T = Value of Demand
r_{Ch} = Audience Costs	r_T = Audience Costs
e_{Ch} = Economic Costs of Exit	e_T = Economic Costs of Exit
$W_{Ch} = v_{Ch} - e_{Ch} - c_{Ch}$	$W_T = v_T - e_T - c_T$
$L_{Ch} = -e_{Ch} - c_{Ch}$	$L_T = -e_T - c_T$

Analysis: A Subgame Perfect Equilibrium Analysis
of the Exit Model

To analyze the equilibrium outcomes of this game, I employ a sequential equilibrium solution concept (Gibbons, 1992; Morrow, 1994). Three equilibria emerge from this analysis: a *constraint equilibrium*, where the costs of exit deter the Challenger from issuing a demand; a *bargaining power equilibrium*, where the costs of exit for the Target allow the Challenger to induce the Target to agree to its demands; and an *escalation equilibrium*, where the use of economic tools of persuasion fails and militarized conflict ensues. Below I discuss the logic that underpins the derivation of these equilibria, and then examine their implications. Since the model is one of complete information, with the exception of the lottery representing the outcome of escalated conflict, we can derive the subgame perfect equilibria using backwards induction (Morrow, 1994).

In this analysis, I make the following assumptions:

- Exit costs for both states are either positive or zero: e_{Ch}, $e_T \geq 0$.
- The value each state associates with the issue at stake in the demand is either positive or zero: V_T, $V_{Ch} \geq 0$.
- Audience costs for the Challenger and audience rewards for the Target are positive: R_{Ch}, $R_T > 0$.

Target's Second Move: Reject or Comply

I begin with the Target's second move, the last move of the game. The Target decides whether to Reject the Challenger's demand or concede. Setting the expected utility of rejecting equal to the expected utility of conceding generates the following:

$$p(-V_T - e_T - c_T) + (1 - p)(-e_T - c_T) = -V_T - e_T. \qquad (3.3)$$

Solving for V_T, the value of the issue at stake for the Target state produces a threshold value, V_T^*, for the Target:

$$V_T^* = \frac{c_T}{1 - p}. \qquad (3.4)$$

The Target rejects the Challenger's demand when $V_T > V_T^*$, and complies when $V_T < V_T^*$.

Challenger's Second Move: Exit or Back Down

The next step is to examine the Challenger's second move in the game. When deciding whether to exit or back down, the Challenger considers the Target's response in the final node of the game tree. If the Challenger backs down, then the Target does not respond, but if the Challenger exits the economic relationship, then the Target can either reject the Challenger a second time or comply with its demands. Case one assumes the Target complies, and Case two assumes it rejects the demand in the final round.

Case One: $V_T < V_T^*$, (Target Complies)

If the Target complies with the Challenger's demands in the final node, the Challenger will receive the value of its demand minus the cost of economic exit, (V_{Ch} - e_{Ch}), by exiting and maintaining its demand. If the Challenger backs down in this case, it pays the audience costs, $-R_{Ch}$. Equation 3.5 sets these utilities equal to one another:

$$V_{Ch} - e_{Ch} = -R_{Ch} . \tag{3.5}$$

Unless the audience costs for the Challenger exceed the net costs of winning compliance and paying exit costs, $R_{Ch} > e_{Ch} - V_{Ch}$, the Challenger will choose to exit when the Target complies.

Case Two: $V_T > V_T^*$, (Target Rejects)

If the Target rejects the Challenger's demands a second time, the Challenger faces a choice between backing down and enduring audience costs or entering into escalated conflict with the Target. The Challenger is indifferent between these two choices when the following equality is satisfied:

$$p(V_{Ch} - e_{Ch} - c_{Ch}) + (1 - p)(-e_{Ch} - c_{Ch}) = -R_{Ch} . \tag{3.6}$$

Let R_{Ch}^* be the threshold of audience costs such that when $R_{Ch}^* > R_{Ch}$, the Challenger backs down. When $R_{Ch}^* < R_{Ch}$, the Challenger exits the economic relationship. Equation 3.7 provides this solution for R_{CH}^* based on equation 3.6:

$$R_{Ch}^* = e_{Ch} + c_{Ch} - pV_{Ch} . \tag{3.7}$$

Thus, this threshold is a function of the costs of economic exit plus the costs of escalation minus the value of the demand and the likelihood of winning the escalated conflict.

Target's First Move: Reject or Comply

There are three cases to be considered by the Target when weighing its options between rejecting the demand made by the Challenger and complying. The first involves the scenario in which the Challenger will back down if the Target rejects the initial demand. The second and third cases deal with a scenario in which the Challenger will exit the economic relationship if the Target rejects the initial demand. In case two, the Target will comply in the second round after the Challenger exits. In case three, the Target rejects the Challenger's demands in both rounds of the game.

Case One: $R_{Ch}^* > R_{Ch}$, (Challenger will Back Down)

Given that the Challenger will back down if the Target rejects its initial demand, the Target faces the following comparison:

$$-V_T < R_T, \text{ for all } V_T, R_T. \tag{3.8}$$

For all possible values of V_T and R_T, the Target will reject this demand if the Challenger will back down in response.

Case Two: $R_{Ch}^* < R_{Ch}$, $V_T < V_T^*$, (Challenger will Exit, Target will Comply)

In this case, since the Target will comply at the second node, after costs of exit have been imposed, it follows that it will also comply in its first move. It faces the following expected utilities comparison:

$$-V_T \geq -V_T - e_T, \text{ for all } V_T, e_T. \tag{3.9}$$

In both outcomes, the Target loses the value it associates with the demand, but in the second round, the Target also pays the cost of the imposed economic exit. Thus, the Target always prefers to comply in the first round (weakly prefers it if $e_T = 0$, strongly prefers otherwise).

Case Three: $R_{Ch}^* < R_{Ch}$, $V_T > V_T^*$, (Challenger will Exit, Target will Reject)

Here the Target faces a Challenger that will exit the economic relationship if the Target rejects the initial demand. If the Target rejects the demand in the first round, it faces escalated conflict. If the Target complies in the first round, it loses the value it associates with the demand. Setting these two expected utilities equal to one another, the Target is indifferent between these two choices when:

$$p(-V_T - e_T - c_T) + (1 - p)(-e_T - c_T) = -V_T . \tag{3.10}$$

Solving for the cost of exit, e_T, equation 3.11 generates an *exit cost threshold* for the Target, e_T^*, which drives its choice between compliance and rejecting the initial demand:

$$e_T^* = (1 - p)V_T - c_T . \tag{3.11}$$

This exit cost threshold is a function of the probability that the Target will win the escalated conflict, the value that it associates with the demand, and the costs the Target incurs in the escalated conflict. When the costs of exit are below this threshold, $e_T < e_T^*$, the Target will reject the demand and escalated conflict will result. When the costs of exit exceed this threshold, $e_T > e_T^*$, the Target cannot afford to endure the costs associated with rejecting the demand. The Target complies with the Challenger's demand at its first opportunity.

Challenger's First Move: Demand or Not Demand

In this first move of the game, the Challenger must weigh the options based on all the possible combinations of choices between itself and the Target. There are three scenarios for the Challenger to consider. In case one, the Target will comply with the initial demand in its first move. In the second and third cases, the Target will reject this initial demand and the Challenger will have to either act on its exit threat or back down. Case two considers the scenario in which the Challenger backs down, and case three considers the scenario in which the Challenger exits and the Target again rejects the demand, with escalated conflict as the outcome. Note that I do not consider here a case where the Target complies in the second round, as it was determined above that the Target will comply in the first round rather than the second.

Case One: $e_T > e_T^*$, (Target will Comply in First Round)

If the Challenger knows that the Target will comply at its first opportunity when faced with a demand, then the Challenger faces two possible outcomes: either it stays at the status quo or it successfully extracts its demand from the Target state. The Challenger will always prefer to extract this demand rather than remain at the status quo (unless it associates a value of zero to the demand, in which case it is indifferent between the two outcomes), as shown in equation 3.12:

$$V_{Ch} \geq 0, \text{ for all } V_{Ch}. \tag{3.12}$$

Case Two: $e_T < e_T^*$, $R_{Ch}^* > R_{Ch}$, (Target Rejects, Challenger Backs Down)

In this scenario, the Challenger knows that if it makes a demand, the Target will reject this demand and the Challenger will then back down. Equation 3.13 shows that the Challenger will always prefer to remain at the status quo in this scenario:

$$-R_{Ch} < 0, \text{ for all } R_{Ch}. \tag{3.13}$$

There is never a scenario in this game in which the Challenger will issue a demand only to back down later.

Case Three: $e_T < e_T^*$, $R_{Ch}^* < R_{Ch}$, (Target Rejects, Challenger Exits, Target Rejects)

Here the Challenger is resolute in its threat of exit, and the Target is resolved to reject the demand. If the Challenger does not make a demand, the status quo results. If the Challenger makes the demand, escalated conflict results. The Challenger is indifferent between these two outcomes when equation 3.14 holds:

$$p(V_{Ch} - e_{Ch} - c_{Ch}) + (1 - p)(-e_{Ch} - c_{Ch}) > 0. \tag{3.14}$$

Solving for the Challenger's exit costs reveals an *exit cost threshold* for the Challenger, e_{Ch}^*, such that,

$$e_{Ch}^* = p(V_{Ch}) - c_{Ch}. \tag{3.15}$$

This threshold behaves in the same way as the exit cost threshold for the Target. The threshold is a function of the likelihood that the Challenger will win the escalated conflict, the value of the issue associated with the demand, and the costs incurred in entering the escalated conflict. When actual exit costs exceed this threshold, $e_{Ch} > e^*_{Ch}$, the Challenger is deterred from making the demand, and the status quo results. When its exit costs fall below this threshold, $e_{Ch} < e^*_{Ch}$, the Challenger makes the demand and escalated conflict ensues. The next section elaborates on the importance of these exit cost thresholds in determining the equilibria for the model.

Exit Cost Thresholds: A Return to the Bargaining Debate

The economic exit costs (e_{Ch} and e_T) and the exit cost thresholds (e^*_{Ch} and e^*_T) show the tipping points for the equilibria.[3] As defined in the analysis above, an exit cost threshold is the level of exit costs beyond which a player cannot endure the exit. Thus, a Challenger whose actual exit costs exceed its exit cost threshold will not move to initiate economic exit in the game. Similarly, a Target state with exit costs that exceed its threshold will accept a demand before the Challenger has a chance to impose this exit.

An exit cost threshold sets a state's limit for exit costs it is willing to bear in order to get (or hold onto) something that another state has (or wants). The model developed here not only posits the existence of these thresholds, it informs us how they are calculated by the states in the game. This is important because we will see below that it is the relationship between a state's actual exit costs and its exit cost threshold that determines whether economic interdependence affects its strategy with respect to political conflict.

For each state, this exit cost threshold is a function of three factors: the value of the demand being made by the Challenger, the costs of escalating to militarized conflict, and the probability that the Challenger or Target will be successful in this high-level conflict. Equations 3.15 and 3.11 define the exit cost thresholds for the Challenger (e^*_{Ch}) and the Target (e^*_T):

$$e^*_{Ch} = pV_{Ch} - c_{Ch} \tag{3.15}$$

$$e^*_T = (1 - p)V_T - c_T. \tag{3.11}$$

The case of Great Britain and Argentina and the Falkland/Malvinas Islands dispute provides an example. Great Britain's threshold is a function of how much it values its possession of the Falkland/Malvinas Islands, how expensive it would be to use military force to reclaim the islands from Argentina, and the likelihood that it would be successful in doing so. Examining the relationship between actual exit costs and exit cost thresholds for the Challenger and Target reveals the following three equilibrium solutions to the model.

When the Challenger's exit costs (e_{Ch}) are greater than its exit cost threshold (e^*_{Ch}), but the Target's exit costs (e_T) are less than its threshold (e^*_T), such that $e_{Ch} > e^*_{Ch}$ and $e_T < e^*_T$, then the Challenger is deterred from making a demand. This is the *constraint equilibrium*, because the Challenger here is constrained by the economic relationship.

When both players' exit costs (e_{Ch}, e_T) are less than their exit cost thresholds (e^*_{Ch}, e^*_T), such that $e_{Ch} < e^*_{Ch}$ and $e_T < e^*_T$, then the Challenger makes a demand, the Target rejects it, the Challenger exits, and the Target again rejects the demand. Conflict escalates, and thus this is the *escalation equilibrium*.

When the Target's exit costs exceed its exit cost threshold, ($e_T > e^*_T$), the Challenger makes a demand and the Target complies. This is the *bargaining power equilibrium*, as the Target's level of interdependence affords the Challenger bargaining power. Note that this equilibrium holds even when the Challenger's exit costs also exceed its own threshold.

Table 3.2 summarizes these results. The equilibria reflect the complexity that exists in the causal link between economic interdependence and conflict. They show that the presence of economic interdependence can generate all three of the interdependence-conflict relationships discussed in chapter 1. The constraint equilibrium is compatible with the argument that economic interdependence reduces conflict because the exit costs that the Challenger faces can prevent it from initiating a demand that leads to conflict. The costs that would result from a loss of the economic ties are sufficient to deter the Challenger from initiating a demand that could lead to low- or high-level conflict.

The bargaining power equilibrium is partially compatible with the argument that economic interdependence generates conflict. In this equilibrium, the Challenger gets what it wants using the threat of exit. These threats and demands can be thought of as low-level conflict, as they are manifestations of a dispute between the two states. In this equilibrium, however, they do not lead to escalated, militarized conflict. Barbieri predicts that asymmetrical economic interdependence will lead to increased militarized conflict. The analysis in this chapter also predicts an increase in conflict, but it is an increase in low-level conflict. This is not to say that the economic interdependence *causes* conflict. The issue involved in the demand is the driving factor in the dispute. The only circumstance in which the economic interaction between two states is the cause of interstate conflict occurs when there is an economic issue motivating the Challenger's demand. This special case aside, the bargaining power equilibrium demonstrates that economic interdependence can *enable* low-level conflict.

Finally, the escalation equilibrium demonstrates that sometimes the economic interdependence is not enough to persuade either side from backing down. In this equilibrium, the economic behavior has no impact on the incidence of conflict (unless an economic issue motivates the initial demand made by the Challenger). This equilibrium occurs when the exit cost thresholds for both states exceed the actual exit costs faced in the game. As such, both states are able to absorb the costs of exit and stand firm, and the economic arena becomes ineffective in resolving the dispute. Several factors can lead to this result. The value states place on the issue at stake may be high enough to push the exit cost thresholds above the actual exit costs. Similarly, if the costs of higher levels of conflict are minimal, then states are less likely to balk at eschewing the economic gloves for military ones. These three equilibria demonstrate that the affect of economic interdependence on political conflict must be assessed within the context of the political and military dimensions of the situation.

Table 3.2. Exit Costs and Equilibrium Behavior

Equilibrium	Strategy for Challenger	Strategy for Target	Exit Cost Threshold
Case One: Constraint	No Demand, Exit if Target Rejects	Reject if Challenger Demands, Reject if Challenger Exits	$e_{Ch}^* < e_{Ch}$, $e_T^* > e_T$
Case Two: Bargaining Power	Demand, Exit if Target Rejects	Comply if Challenger Demands	$e_T^* < e_T$
Case Three: Escalation	Demand, Exit if Target Rejects	Reject if Challenger Demands, Reject if Challenger Exits	$e_{Ch}^* > e_{Ch}$, $e_T^* > e_T$

Revisiting Asymmetry

Wagner was correct in arguing that asymmetry in interdependence, defined as unequal levels of dependence within the dyad, is insufficient to
generate bargaining power for the less dependent state. The Target could
have a much higher level of economic dependence than the Challenger,
but if the Target's exit costs are lower than its exit cost threshold, then
the economic relationship is useless for the Challenger. Similarly, the
Target could have a much lower exit cost than the Challenger, but if the
Target's exit costs exceed its threshold, the Target will yield to the Challenger's demands. Raw exit cost levels do not provide enough information to determine whether economic interdependence will help or hinder
the Challenger.

This is not to say that asymmetry in interdependence is insignificant.
If we consider the dyadic relationship with respect to who has exit costs

exceeding their thresholds and who does not, then the concept of asymmetry has explanatory value. For example, if the Challenger faces exit costs that are below its exit cost threshold, but the Target faces exit costs that are above its threshold, there exists an asymmetry in the interdependence that is meaningful. If both states are above or below their respective thresholds, then the interdependence is symmetrical.

This generates a new interpretation of symmetry in interdependence. Symmetry with respect to each state's exit cost to cost-threshold relationship determines the presence or absence of bargaining power. The analysis also indicates that symmetry is not always an important factor in determining the influence interdependence has on conflict. Figure 3.3 displays how this symmetry in the cost-threshold relationships affects the equilibrium outcomes of the game. The vertical axis represents the actual exit costs for the Target, and the horizontal axis represents the exit costs for the Challenger. Hypothetical exit cost thresholds have been inserted along these axes, and using these thresholds the two-dimensional space divided into the four possible combinations of exit costs and thresholds for both players.

Figure 3.3. Symmetry in Exit Costs and Thresholds

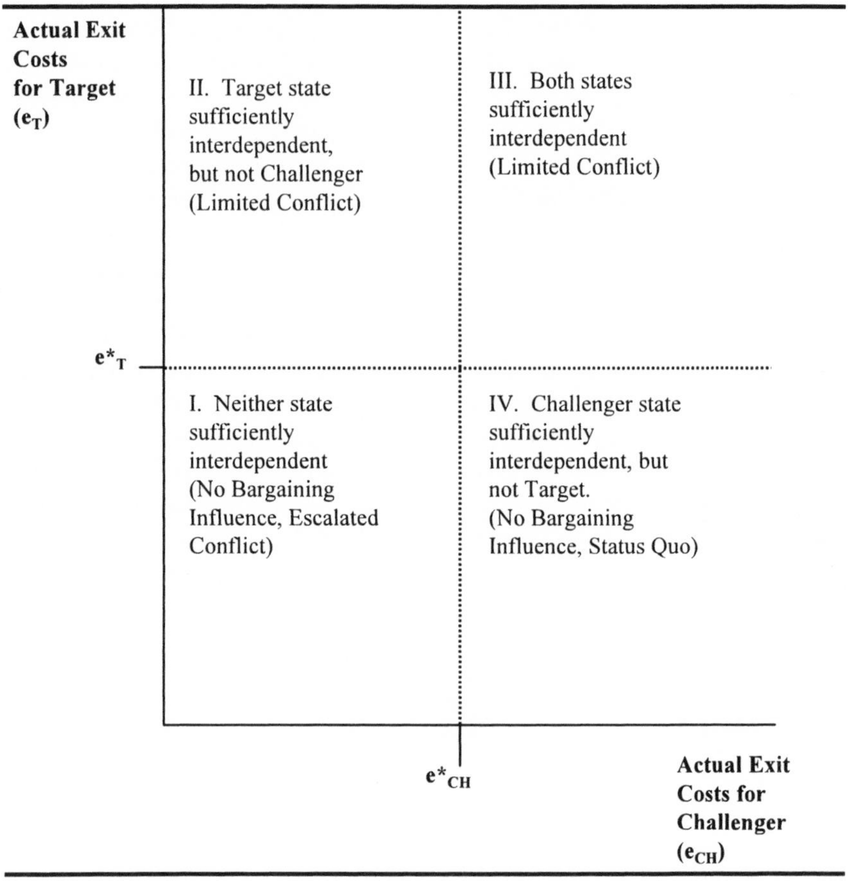

Actual Exit Costs for Target (e_T)	II. Target state sufficiently interdependent, but not Challenger (Limited Conflict)	III. Both states sufficiently interdependent (Limited Conflict)
e^*_T	I. Neither state sufficiently interdependent (No Bargaining Influence, Escalated Conflict)	IV. Challenger state sufficiently interdependent, but not Target. (No Bargaining Influence, Status Quo)
	e^*_{CH}	**Actual Exit Costs for Challenger (e_{CH})**

Quadrant I, in the bottom left corner of the graph, represents the situation when neither state faces exit costs exceeding its cost threshold. Bargaining is not effective, and the Challenger is not constrained. In the event of a dispute between the Challenger and Target, economic interdependence will not constrain the dyad from escalating to high-levels of conflict. Quadrant II, in the top left corner of the graph, represents the situation where the Challenger faces exit costs that fall below its threshold but the Target's exit costs exceed its threshold. In this situation, the Challenger has bargaining power by manipulating the Target's economic dependence, and low-level conflict results. The same result obtains in quadrant III, in the top right corner, where both states face exit costs which exceed their thresholds. Thus, the difference in symmetry between II and III has no effect on the outcome of the model. Symmetry is important, however, in comparing quadrant IV to I or III. In quadrant IV, in the bottom right corner of the graph, the Challenger's exit costs exceed its threshold, but the Target's costs do not. As such, the Challenger is constrained by economic interdependence from initiating a demand that could lead to conflict. The differences in symmetry between quadrants IV and I and quadrants IV and III have an important effect on the outcome of the model.

Conclusion

The exit model developed in this chapter is a simple theory of interstate interaction. Several of the assumptions underlying the model can be relaxed to make the model more realistic and complex. For example, we can relax the assumption that the value each state associates with the demand (V_{Ch}, V_T) is public information. Since this information is key to the derivation of exit cost thresholds (see equations 3.11, 3.15), allowing one or both states to hold private information in this way obscures the opponent's view of the exit cost to cost threshold relationship. This introduces the opportunity for states to bluff. A Challenger may threaten economic exit even when its exit costs exceed its thresholds while the Target's do not. A Target may reject the Challenger's initial demand although it faces exit costs that exceed the Target's exit cost threshold. These strategies are plausible in a world of incomplete information regarding exit cost thresholds. With assumptions of complete information in place, however, the model predicts that states will not incur economic exit except in situations where high-level conflict ensues. The logic is clear: if both states have complete information about the other state's threshold levels, then they know a priori whether economic exit will be effective. If a Challenger knows that the Target faces exit costs that fall beneath its threshold, then the Challenger will only initiate a demand if it is prepared to escalate the conflict to high levels. In the real world, we observe economic exit without high-level conflict (i.e., the United States grain embargo against the USSR in 1979). This behavior is off the equilibrium path in the exit model developed above; either due to error in the decision makers in the real world, or due to an artifact of an assumption in the model that does not hold in all situations. This second explanation suggests that future research should begin with this generalization of the exit model to incorporate incomplete information in the economic relationship.

This does not take away, however, from the progress that has been gained by establishing the basic exit model. By explicitly modeling the role of economic exit in political decision making, I have specified the complex relationship between economic interdependence and political conflict. This model provides a platform for more focused empirical research. The next two chapters employ qualitative and quantitative research methods to assess the exit model's performance in furthering our understanding of economic interdependence and political conflict in the real world.

Notes

1. See Harsanyi (1977: 186-89).
2. One such drawback that will become clear in the following text is that game theory performs best when models are highly abstract. As one adds more detail and structure to a game, its analysis quickly becomes intractable. There are other dimensions of the game structure employed in this chapter that can be expanded upon in future research. For example, one could try to capture the long-term effects of using threats to extract demands, or reduce the current reliance on heroic assumptions such as treating nations as unitary actors or assuming complete information among nations.
3. As the payoffs of this game are a function of the cost and benefit parameters, the researcher has flexibility in terms of solving for a specific parameter. My decision to focus on the exit cost parameter is driven by the substantive interests of this study, but one could just as easily center the analysis around the probability of winning a militarized conflict (p), or the value of the issue at stake (v).

4

Assessing the Exit Model in the Real World

With the theoretical framework and analysis in place, the next step is to apply chapter 3's equilibrium predictions to the empirical world. Chapters 2 and 3 established economic interdependence as a function of potential economic exit costs and developed a model of how this interdependence can deter, motivate, or fail to affect political conflict. Now we are ready to see how concept and theory serve us by providing a lens with which to view the real world.

To this end, below I examine three cases that illustrate the equilibria of the exit model: constraint, bargaining power, and escalation. The case of the United States and South Africa during the Apartheid era illustrates the constraint equilibrium. This case focuses on the reluctance of the United States to use its position as the leading export market for South Africa as a bargaining tool to encourage the end of Apartheid. As an illustration, it is useful because it provides an example of how economic interdependence can deter a Challenger from making demands that could escalate into military conflict. It also demonstrates how market structure and adaptation costs drive exit costs, and it shows us how basic trade data can generate misleading predictions regarding interdependence. Finally, it provides an example of the distinction between economic sanctions and economic exit.[1]

The relationship between China and the United States from 1989 to 1998 illustrates the bargaining power equilibrium, and it too demonstrates that trade data can incorrectly represent exit costs. This case focuses on the value of U.S. access to China's growing market. While current trade levels suggest that China is the more dependent state, its market potential for the next decade has U.S. business interests bending over backwards to gain a foothold. China used this position to extract advanced technology from the United States, including technology that can serve both military and commercial needs, despite a ban on such technology transfer by the United States in response to the Tiananmen Square Incident.

The third case focuses on Great Britain and Argentina in 1982 to illustrate the escalation equilibrium. This case demonstrates the limits of economic interdependence in deterring conflict. Argentina's forceful invasion of the Malvinas Islands in April of 1982 sparked a new round of this historical crisis. Domestic issues within each state enhanced the political value of the Malvinas Islands, which in turn raised the exit cost thresholds. Neither state faced high exit costs. For Great Britain, these low exit costs facilitated the threat and subsequent imposition of sanctions against Argentina in an attempt to convince Galtieri to abandon Argentina's claim to the Malvinas Islands. These low exit costs also allowed Argentina to stand firm in their new position on the islands despite British sanctioning efforts.

Table 4.1 summarizes the three equilibria of the exit model in substantive terms and establishes the necessary conditions for each equilibrium. The focus throughout this chapter will be on whether real exit costs exceeded or fell below the exit cost thresholds faced by each state. While the actual thresholds are impossible to identify, the evidence seeks to shed light on whether the actors perceived themselves to be facing exit costs that fall above or below what they consider tolerable costs.

Methodological Issues

As these case histories are intended to serve as illustrations of the theoretical model, they were not selected using the guidelines of research design, nor do they constitute a test of the model. The goal of this chapter is to use the exit model as a lens through which we can assess real-world behavior. The narrative method is useful to accomplish this goal because it allows the researcher to study the sequence of events and the strategic interaction of the case. The theoretical model can be applied on the whole to each case, providing a richer look at the model than alternative methods such as large-n analysis. Of particular importance here is the ability to flesh out the costs and benefits each nation faces in the exit model as well as evidence of whether one or both states faced exit costs that exceeded their cost thresholds.

This focus on a small set of cases provides non-mathematical representations of the exit model while demonstrating the importance of the role of exit costs and economic interdependence in international relations. Such an approach escapes the research design problem of identifying the universe of available cases relating to the equilibria in the theoretical model. This problem affects many game theoretic models where the structure of the game allows actors to choose not to act at all and remain at the status quo. For example, the exit model generates three equilibria. Identifying the universe of cases with respect to the equilibria would result in varying degrees of difficulty. The universe of cases pertaining to the escalation equilibrium is small and easily identifiable due to the presence of military conflict. The universe of cases involving the threat of exit without military conflict is also obtainable in theory, although it is considerably larger in size and issues of underreporting and missing data are problematic. It would be extremely difficult, however, to identify the universe of cases associated with the constraint equilibrium. The decision by the Challenger to not make a demand and thus keep the state of relations at the status quo is an important part of the exit model, but its predicted outcome represents an infinite class of behavior in international relations. Selected qualitative case histories avoid these research design problems, but there are costs associated with this strategy as well as benefits.

The narratives presented here represent an empirical assessment of the model in that they are important cases in world politics involving both economic and political dimensions of the interstate relationships. If the exit model can provide new information that improves our understanding of why the events in these cases happened the way they did, then the cases support the exit model as a tool of social science. This assessment, however, cannot be considered a test of the model for the simple reason that the cases were selected to match the predicted outcomes of the equilibria. An interesting puzzle also motivated the selection of these cases. In each case, the basic trade relationships provide misleading

Table 4.1. Constraint, Bargaining Power, and Escalation Equilibria

Equilibrium	Outcome	Necessary Condition	Case	Description
1. **Constraint** (Challenger is constrained from making demands)	**Status Quo**: No demand made by Challenger	Challenger's exit costs exceed its exit cost threshold, but Target's do not.	U.S. and South Africa: Apartheid Era 1962 to 1989. *Challenger*: U.S. *Target*: South Africa	U.S. vetoes many UN resolutions for sanctions, never cuts strategic minerals imports from South Africa.
2. **Bargaining Power** (Challenger can safely, successfully make demands)	**Low-level, Non-militarized Conflict**: Challenger demands, Target acquiesces.	Target's exit costs exceed its exit cost threshold.	China and U.S.: Technology Transfer to China 1989 to present. *Challenger*: China *Target*: U.S.	China demands "dual-use" technology transfers from the U.S. despite ban. China uses the threat of refusing access to its huge domestic market as a bargaining tool.
3. **Escalation** (Threat and exit ineffective)	**Militarized Conflict**: Challenger demands, Target rejects, Challenger exits, Target rejects again, conflict escalates.	Neither Challenger's nor Target's exit costs exceed thresholds.	Great Britain (G.B.) and Argentina: 1982 Malvinas Conflict. *Challenger*: G.B. *Target*: Argentina	G.B. fails in its attempt to use economic sanctions to persuade Argentina to move troops off Malvinas Islands. Conflict escalates, G.B. uses force to reclaim islands.

information about the exit costs and thus the economic interdependence between the two states. In short, they are good candidates to highlight the logic of the exit model while demonstrating that the current focus on trade in the literature is problematic.

Recently scholars have visited the issue of the utility of small-n case studies in assessing formal models (Alston et al., 1996; Huber, 1996; Bates et al., 1998). These scholars agree that it is misguided to try to equate small-n and large-n approaches in terms of research design (see King et al., 1994). Instead, we need to appreciate the strengths and weaknesses of the small-n approach with respect to empirical work based on formal models. The strength of the case study approach lies in its ability to extract details and sequencing from the historical narrative that allow us to study the plausibility and logic of the formal model in its entirety. In a discussion of the utility of qualitative analysis in highlighting the logic and structure of formal models, Huber argues:

> . . . careful study of these details can bring into sharp relief the fundamental motivations and constraints on actions that guide the choices of individuals in particular classes of events. It is the logic of the argument rather than the validity of its empirical claims that makes a qualitative case study compelling (1996: 141).

Alston suggests that case studies can serve as an effective empirical tool in assessing the logical consistency of a model (1996: 30). Presenting an approach labeled as "analytic narratives," Bates et al. argue that the historical narrative and abstract theory should be intertwined such that each is informed by the other (1998: 10-13).

The agenda for this chapter is similar to the analytic narratives approach, but it differs in two ways. First, while the cases highlight both strengths and weaknesses in the logical structure and plausibility of the exit model, the formal model is not customized to fit each case. Rather, here the cases are fit to the model. One of the advantages of having a formal model is that the reader can have some sense of the perceptions of the author when reading the following historical accounts. Every case study is generated with a template in mind (explicitly or implicitly), and one of the greatest strengths of formal modeling is the transparency of this template that the model provides for the researcher and the scholarly community for this template to be made transparent. Huber argues for the use of formal models as guides in case study analysis:

Qualitative case studies have the advantage of treating structures and motivations as endogenous, but without a tool for formally specifying assumptions about behavior and strategic interaction, it is difficult to base one's evaluation of the logical correctness of the story on more than intuition and informed judgment of the author's selection and arrangement of qualitative detail. And without theoretical guidance of some sort, the qualitative researcher will never know which details to latch onto and bring to the fore in his or her theory (1996: 142).

Second, in analytic narratives the explanation of the case is the primary agenda, and the formal model serves as a tool for generating a unique explanation. In this chapter the agenda is to gain a better understanding of the exit model, using the cases as tools to communicate and evaluate the structure and analysis of the theory. Huber, however, inadvertently highlights the danger in attributing too much weight to case studies. With or without "theoretical guidance" the qualitative researcher must sift through an immense (indeed, infinite) body of information in preparing his or her case. The combination of this subjectivity in the collection and presentation of evidence and the lack of research design in the selection of cases suggests that one should be hard pressed to *not* find cases which support one's theories. This is not to say that small-n, qualitative analysis is not an important tool in the evaluation of theory. Rather, while case histories excel in providing rich detail and assessment of theory, this assessment is only valid internally for the case employed in the analysis, and care should be taken not to generalize the empirical support (or lack thereof).

Inevitably, when case histories are employed to demonstrate the empirical relevance of abstract theory, the results are mixed. Thus, while the cases in this chapter succeed in illustrating the utility and novelty of the exit model, they also challenge its assumptions of states as unitary actors and the issue of what degree of economic manipulation constitutes economic exit. With this perspective in mind, the first illustration of the exit model is a case that fits the constraint equilibrium path. The case of the United States and South Africa demonstrates how economic interdependence can constrain even the most powerful of states from pursuing their desired political strategies.

Constraint: The United States, South Africa, and Apartheid

During the decades in which a small minority of white South Africans ruled with a repressive government over a nation with a vast majority of black South Africans, the world repeatedly called for the end of Apartheid. The United Nations, the European Community, and even the United States imposed economic sanctions of various degrees upon South Africa in protest of Apartheid, with very little success. Despite this apparent show of force, no state or institution ever imposed a comprehensive ban on imports of strategic minerals from South Africa. Combined with the fact that in 1980, for example, exports of these strategic minerals represented 76 percent of South Africa's foreign exchange earnings,[2] what appeared to be a show of force in retrospect looks more like a meager attempt to manipulate South African domestic policy. Indeed, the two "sanctions" applied by the United States against South Africa during the Apartheid era resulted in an annual per capita cost of $0.08 and $17.19 to South Africans (Hufbauer et al., 1990b).

Any serious effort to use the economic ties between the two states as a political bargaining tool for the United States would have to involve South Africa's strategic minerals exports. Yet, the United States never threatened to exit this most salient dimension of the economic relationship. In this section, I examine the actions of the United States with the use of the exit model to see if U.S. strategy was rational given its economic relationship with South Africa. Here I define the United States as the Challenger, and South Africa as the Target. By applying the framework of the exit model to this case, I conclude that the United States was constrained from making a serious threat of exit from its core economic relationship with South Africa. The costs that the United States would have faced from economic exit were extraordinarily high, and global demand for strategic minerals meant low exit costs for South Africa. As such, the equilibrium strategy for the United States was to avoid the use of economic exit to impose its demand that South Africa end Apartheid.

Cost-Benefit Analysis

One could assume that the Civil Rights movement in the United States serves as evidence that the United States desired to see the end of Apartheid. Those who would shy away from granting the United States such humanitarian character need only look at the economic interests of U.S. banks and corporations that would benefit from the reduced investment risk resulting from the end of Apartheid to conclude that the end of Apartheid was in the best economic interest of the United States. Chase Manhattan Bank, for example, ceased its lending to South Africa in 1985, citing the increased risk in the investments. Two weeks later, the rand (South Africa's currency) dropped twenty percent in value after Prime Minister Botha attributed domestic disturbances to "barbaric communist agitators" (Hufbauer et al., 1990b: 223).

Using either logic, if one assumes that the United States had an interest in ending Apartheid, then why did it not choose to use its superior economic weight to impose this political demand upon South Africa? Specifically, why did the United States continually veto UN resolutions for mandatory sanctions, and why did the United States never institute an embargo of South Africa's most valuable exports: strategic minerals? Figure 4.1 demonstrates that the trade relationship, in terms of monetary value, is skewed the way we would anticipate; the imports and exports between the United States and South Africa often make up roughly 20 percent or more of South Africa's total trade, but never more than 3 percent of that of the United States. As the richer and seemingly less dependent state, the arguments set forth by Hirschman and Keohane & Nye suggest that the United States should have had the ability to manipulate this economic relationship and demand that South Africa alter its domestic policy by ending Apartheid. A closer look at the economic relationship and the market structure within which it exists, however, reveals a very different picture.

South Africa's economy in the post-World War II era has been driven primarily by its sale of minerals to the rest of the world. It has long relied on its mineral wealth to obtain the few goods it needs to import: oil, military technology, and capital. Thus, any state that sought to use economic means to convince South Africa to end Apartheid should have targeted mineral exports. Why, then, did the United States never threaten to exit the economic relationship with South Africa, specifically its purchases of South Africa's minerals? Even the Comprehensive Anti-Apartheid Act of 1986 passed by the United States Congress (vetoed by President Reagan, but overridden by Congress) excludes strategic minerals from the list of sanctions (Hufbauer et al., 1990b: 227-8). The answer lies in the actual exit costs that the United States and South Africa would face in the event of such a comprehensive economic exit.

South Africa has the world's largest known deposits of chromium, manganese, and platinum despite occupying less than 1 percent of the earth's land surface. Chromium and manganese are essential to the production of steel, and platinum is used as a catalytic agent to refine petroleum and reduce automobile emissions. These minerals are considered essential not only to the United States, but to Europe as well (SCUSPTSA, 1981: 310).

The strategic importance of these minerals lies in their use as well as their availability. Chromium, in the processed form of chromium ferroalloy, is needed in the production of stainless and heat-resisting steel, full-alloy steel, and superalloys (U.S. Geological Survey, 1973-1996). Similarly, manganese is a necessary hardening agent in the production of steel. These metals were used extensively throughout the post-World War II era, as well as today, in the production of jet engines and power plant equipment. Superalloys have also been used in the pursuit of stronger, lighter defense equipment (SCUSPTSA, 1981: 311-15). Platinum's main uses have been in the automotive (catalytic converters), chemical, and petroleum-refining industries.

Figure 4.1. Trade between the United States and South Africa

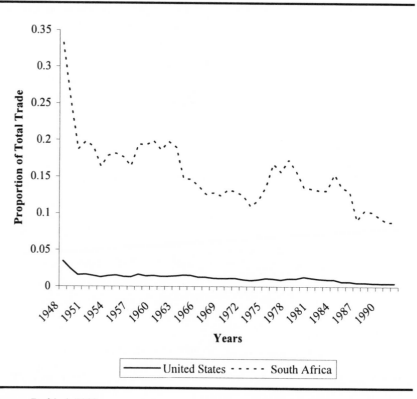

Source: Barbieri, 1999

Three other factors establish the exit costs the United States would have endured during a comprehensive economic exit. First, alternative supplies of chromium, manganese, and platinum were hard to come by, especially during the Cold War. Figure 4.2 shows the world's reserves for these three minerals in 1983. Not only did South Africa possess over 77 percent of the reserves for these minerals; the second largest supplier was the Soviet Union.[3] Thus, South African dominance in the minerals market generated market imperfections that would increase the exit costs faced by the United States. Compounding this effect was the lack of U.S. domestic capacity to produce the minerals.

Figure 4.2. Mineral Reserves (Chromium, Manganese, and Platinum, 1983)

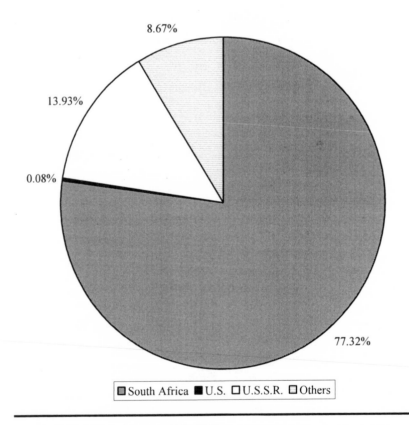

Source: U.S. Geological Survey, 1973-1996

The reliance of the United States on imports for chromium, manganese, and platinum minerals from 1973 to 1996 appears in figure 4.3. The United States imported 100 percent of its chromium ore consumption, but used some of this ore to produce ferrochrome for domestic use. The data series for chromium in figure 4.3 reflects this partial domestic production. Even with this domestic production of ferrochrome the United States relied on imports for at least 79 percent of its chromium demands throughout the post-World War II period. Manganese imports represent 97 to 100 percent of U.S. consumption, and platinum imports varied from 81 to 94 percent. The United States would be unable to produce enough of these minerals to satisfy its own demand in the event that the South African supply was not available. Finally, the third factor driving up exit costs for the United States was a lack of substitutability for these minerals. No effective substitute exists for the use of chromium and manganese in steel production, and substitute minerals for platinum in catalyst functions are still experimental (U.S. Geological Survey, 1973-1996).

These four factors—the reliance of the United States on the minerals, the monopolistic power of South Africa in their supply, the inability of the United States to produce the minerals domestically, and the lack of substitutes—result in deep exit costs for the United States. The first factor reveals that the United States-South African economic relationship was much more salient to the United States than indicated by the overall trade data. The second factor highlights the advantage provided to the South Africans by the market structure for these strategic minerals. The last two factors suggest that the United States faced the problem of high asset specificity concerning the minerals. Figure 4.4 provides the proportion of total U.S. imports of chromium, manganese, and platinum from South Africa from 1973 to 1996. Examining the chromium import data indicates that the United States was at its peak dependence (64 percent of all chromium imports) on South Africa during the mid-1980s, when the Apartheid debate was center stage. Reagan's boosting of defense spending to attempt to outpace the Soviets in the Cold War arms race meant that stainless steel and superalloys were in high demand, thus creating exit costs for the United States that were prohibitively high.

While it is impossible to know exactly where the exit cost threshold for the United States was during this time, it seems safe to conclude that the exit costs it faced in the event of comprehensive sanctions against South Africa exceeded this threshold. The United States was not alone in this situation. Major powers such as Great Britain, West Germany, and Japan all faced a similar relationship with South Africa, and these countries had even less storage capacity to endure sanctions. Despite frequent calls from the UN for more action, none of the major powers of the Western world were able or willing to absorb the costs involved with true economic exit from their ties with South Africa.

Figure 4.3. U.S. Reliance on Imports of Three Key Minerals

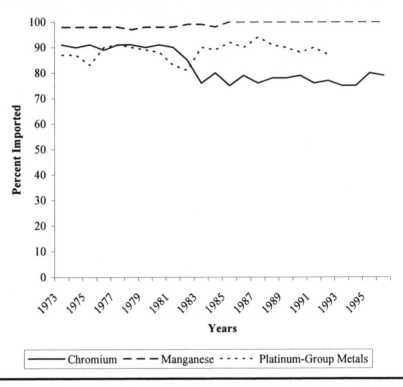

Source: U.S. Geological Survey, 1973-1996

Here I would like to examine this case from the perspective of the exit model. Let the United States be the Challenger and South Africa the Target. The "lunch money" in this case is the practice of Apartheid, in that the United States wants South Africa to give it up but South Africa wants to preserve it. Finally, let the "lab partnership" in this case be the sale of strategic minerals by South Africa to the United States. Using this perspective, let us examine the fit of the strategies of the United States and South Africa to the equilibrium predictions of the exit model. The analysis in chapter 3 indicates that even if the Challenger faces exit costs that exceed its threshold, it can still successfully use the threat of exit to obtain its demands if the Target also faces exit costs that exceed its own threshold.

Examining the impact of a U.S. economic exit on South Africa shows that this was not the case. As the world's leading supplier of strategic minerals, South Africa had many alternative buyers. Great Britain also imported the vast majority of its demand of these minerals and maintained substantial economic relations with South Africa throughout the Apartheid era (Anti-Apartheid Movement Report, 1986). Virtually any free-world country engaged in the production of steel or products requiring the use of steel (Japan and West Germany being two of the largest consumers outside the United States) had to go to South Africa for the necessary chromium and manganese. This is not to say that economic exit by the United States would not have been costly for South Africa; however, their monopoly position in the minerals market combined with a broad demand for these minerals assured them that the exit costs imposed by the United States would be relatively low.

While these potential exit costs for South Africa were low, the value that the South African government placed on maintaining its domestic policies was high. The South African government denounced the idea of majority rule for the simple reason that they feared the repression it would bring upon the white minority (Hufbauer et al., 1990b: 233). After over four decades of repressing blacks, the white minority held considerable fears regarding retribution by a black majority in power. Based on the combination of low exit costs and a high value associated with maintaining the status quo, I conclude here that in the event of a demand to end Apartheid and a threat of economic exit by the United States, the South African government was willing to bear the costs of economic exit.

Figure 4.4. U.S. Reliance on South Africa for Imports

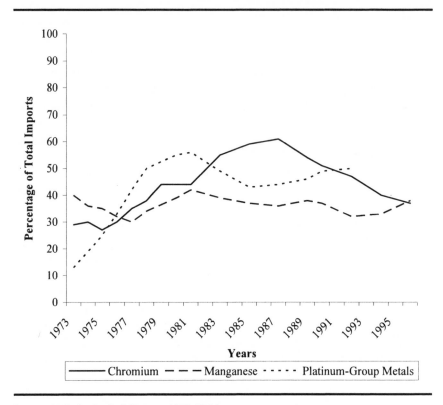

Source: U.S. Geological Survey, 1973-1996

Assessing the Performance of the Exit Model

Given that the Challenger in this case faced exit costs that exceeded its exit cost threshold, and the Target faced exit costs that fell below its threshold, the analysis in chapter 3 predicts that the Challenger will forego its opportunity to issue a demand and threaten economic exit. The relations between the United States and South Africa throughout the 1960's, 1970's, and 1980's illustrate this constraint equilibrium (see figure 4.5). The United States repeatedly vetoed UN resolutions for mandatory sanctions against South Africa. The Johnson administration refused to form a systematic policy for South Africa (David, 1982). The Carter administration had data compiled on U.S. vulnerability to mineral imports from South Africa and concluded that non-intervention was in the best interest of his economy (Beukes, 1987). In 1981, President Reagan instituted a policy of "constructive engagement" with South Africa, citing the inability of the United States to successfully use economic force to coerce the South African government (Hufbauer et al., 1990b: 221-35). Despite repeated calls for sanctions both from within the United States and anti-Apartheid groups around the world, the United States knew that economic exit would fail to bring about change in South Africa. The costs of exit for the United States precluded military options as well, and its only viable option was to accept the status quo.

Figure 4.5. U.S.-South Africa Constraint Equilibrium

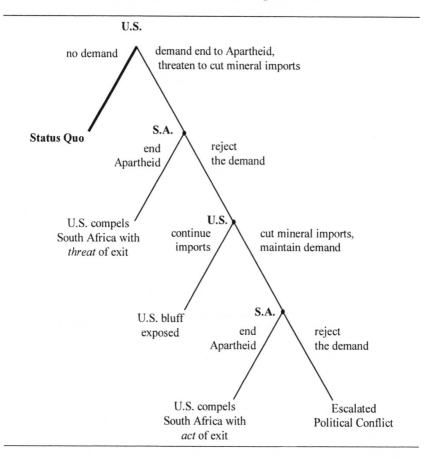

This case also highlights a shortcoming of the model. Specifically, it reveals the difficulty one faces when trying to determine what exactly represents economic exit. After all, the United States did impose and maintain economic sanctions upon South Africa throughout this period. Where do we draw the line between token sanctions and economic exit? Another problem of the model is its inability to account for compromise between the two states. For example, South Africa frequently made small concessions on human rights in an attempt to satisfy U.S. demands without ending Apartheid. The model forces the Target into a simple accept-reject choice, and the empirical world is often more subtle than this dichotomy.

The next case turns the tables and examines the role of the United States as a Target rather than Challenger. Just as economic interdependence can constrain major powers from making demands upon smaller and less powerful (militarily) states, it can also make a major power state vulnerable to political manipulation. Below I examine how China has been able to exploit its economic relationship with the United States to extract technology despite a U.S. ban on technology transfer.

Bargaining Power: China, the United States, and Military Technology

In June of 1989, when the standoff in Tiananmen Square boiled over and the Chinese government violently repressed the student movement, the United States reacted swiftly by ceasing arms sales and military contacts with China. Public outcry against China was intense in the United States, as Congress pushed the administration to administer strong sanctions. Some wondered if selling arms to China would come back to haunt the United States in a future conflict. The U.S. government responded to the incident by banning military arms and technology exports to China.

Just four days after the Chinese military clashed with students in the square and the Bush administration in the United States imposed the ban on military exports, however, Bush reaffirmed his decision to extend Most Favored Nation status (MFN) to China. This decision indicated to the world that economic exit was not a tool the United States was willing to use in an effort to demand improved human rights in China. Rather, the decision to restrict the flow of arms sales to China resulted from a loss of confidence in China's progress towards a more liberal society. These new export controls had no time limit, and the U.S. administration and Congress seemed resolved that this was the proper course of action. Almost a decade later, these controls remain (at least on paper). In short, the United States was not using these sanctions as economic leverage to encourage China to improve its domestic human rights policies. The United States revised its status quo behavior with China based on the events at hand in order to prevent contributing to China's military development.

From the beginning of this new policy, however, the United States has had trouble with enforcement of this new status quo. In July of 1989, President Bush approved an exception to the export controls and allowed the sale to China of three Boeing jets containing Honeywell navigation systems that are considered "dual-use" technology (commercial and military) (Hufbauer et al., 1990b: 270). In December 1989, Bush also waived export controls on three American-made satellites (272). The Clinton administration continued where Bush left off, making exceptions to the export policies in the hopes of opening opportunities for U.S. business in the coming years in China. When the military in China began using American-made satellites originally sold and launched for commercial use, the Clinton administration maintained that if the United States had not provided the satellites, China would have obtained them from Europe (Gerth, 1998).

Over the last decade, technology transfer from the United States to China has rapidly increased, often blurring the line between military and commercial use. During this time the United States and its corporations have faced increasing demands from China for the transfer of technology as a requirement for access to China's market (Sanger, 1996). Technology transfer is defined here as the "methods by which technologies, expertise, or know-how can be transferred from one party or state to another" (Bureau of Export Administration [BXA], 1999: 1). Some examples of technology transfer include the sharing of product designs and patents, employee training, or equipment designed to produce the export product (BXA, 1999: 2). Despite the hard line the United States tried to take in 1989, more often than not it finds itself giving in to the demands for technology. What has driven the United States to make so many compromises against its 1989 policy on exports to China?

To shed light on this puzzle, I apply the exit model to these historical events. China is defined as the Challenger in this game, with the United States as the Target. The demand being made by China is for the transfer of "dual-use" technology that can easily be adapted for military use. This technology transfer violates the principle of the export controls imposed by the United States in response to the Tiananmen Square incident.

China employs a threat of economic exit to add leverage to its demands. Economic exit in this case is the revocation or limitation of U.S. access to the massive and relatively untapped domestic economy of China.

Cost-Benefit Analysis

As in the U.S.-South Africa case, the predictions that emerge from a focus on absolute or relative trade levels are inconsistent with the observed behavior by the United States and China. Figure 4.6 indicates that China's reliance on U.S.-China trade is much more intense than that of the United States, suggesting that the United States should have been able to take advantage of this asymmetry and maintain its policy of export controls. Instead, China is increasingly dictating the terms of economic interaction. Using the analysis in chapter 3 and the rational expectations argument set forth by Dale Copeland (1996), I argue here that the exit costs the United States would incur by not giving in to China's demands were prohibitive. With the predicted market for Chinese imports already in the hundreds of millions of dollars and climbing every year, the potential in China in the coming years has proven to be irresistible to U.S. business (Barfield, 1994). Can the strategies of China and the United States be considered rational, at least with respect to the exit model?

The key to this puzzle lies in the exit costs of the Target. The behavior of China and the United States in this scenario fits the *bargaining power equilibrium* as it is primarily a function of the exit costs and the exit cost threshold of the Target. That is, if the Target (the United States) faces exit costs that exceed its exit cost threshold, then the Challenger (China) can successfully extract demands from the Target even if its own exit costs are also high.

Using the language of the exit model, let us recast this scenario. Beginning from the premise that the 1989 export controls are in place and considered permanent by all parties, I assume that this situation represents the status quo. China, as the Challenger, seeks to change the status quo in order to extract advanced technology from the United States. The United States, as the Target, seeks to preserve its position as the world leader in technology. It worries that any technology transfer will erode that position and generate security problems if China employs such technology for military use. In this case, technology transfer is the "lunch money." Let us also assume here that since the Chinese economy is still quite centralized, and the export policies of 1989 require the U.S. Department of Commerce to examine and approve technology transfers to China, we can consider both nations in this scenario as unitary actors.

Figure 4.6. Trade between the United States and China as a Proportion of Total Trade

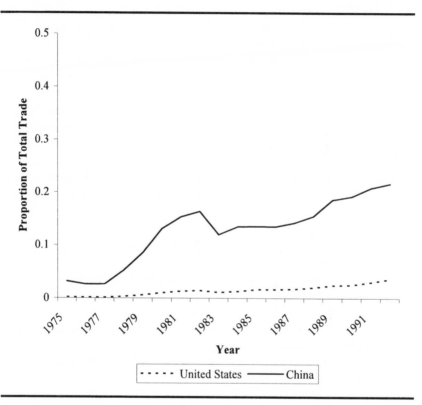

Source: Barbieri, 2002

The threat involved in this case (the "lab partnership") is the U.S. access to Chinese markets. Whereas in the first case we were concerned with specific goods (minerals), here the economic relationship is the broader issue of whether each side will be able to export goods to the other. Recent research suggests that when weighing the interdependence of an economic relationship, nations assess not only the present economic situation, but also future relationships (Copeland, 1996). While many United States firms have yet to make a profit in their dealings in

China, the potential demand and sheer size of China's market cannot be ignored.

China's goal in this game is to use this access to their future market to extract technology demands from the United States, ideally without paying the costs of losing access to its primary source of exports, the U.S. market. So far, it has been remarkably successful. One of the best examples of this situation is the sale of Boeing aircraft:

> When Boeing or other aircraft makers sell a plane to China, Beijing insists they spend as much as a third of the money received buying Chinese parts, or handing over the technology to make those parts. (Smith and Hamilton, 1995: A14)

This situation has generated a dilemma for the U.S. government, as these demands for aircraft technology "are forcing Washington to choose between losing a deal and aiding Beijing's efforts to build both commercial aircraft and, in the view of some, long-range bombers" (Sanger, 1996: 1). Boeing is not alone in its push in Washington to allow such concessions. A report issued by the U.S. Department of Commerce finds that the practice is widespread and even institutionalized in business with China:

> The transfer of advanced U.S. technology is the price of market access in China for U.S. high-tech companies. . . . Technology transfer is . . . mandated in Chinese regulations or industrial policies (with which U.S. companies wishing to invest in China must comply). (BXA, 1999: v)

The demands of China are clear. Technology transfer must take place, or market access will be revoked or denied. Given that the United States has been the superior economic power throughout this period, what explains China's success in obtaining technology?

The United States strongly prefers to prevent technology transfers from occurring as the potential costly effects include loss of American jobs (especially in high wage earning high-technology sectors, loss of capital, and the enhancement of foreign competition) (BXA, 1999: 2). In addition to these long-run economic costs, there is concern that providing China with technology that can find its way into its military may present future problems for U.S. national security (Mahnken, 1996; Sanger, 1996).

Despite these costs, the costs of losing out on access to China's market appear to be higher:

The potential of China's market is simply unparalleled, and the prospect of selling most anything to over one billion people, in one place, is irresistible. (BXA, 1999: 45)

As such, China's potential markets have generated monopsony power for China at the bargaining table. The value of access to this potential wealth outweighs the political and economic costs involved with giving in to China's demands. In addition, being blocked from Chinese markets will put U.S. corporations at a significant disadvantage in the global marketplace, as competition for access to China's market has become increasingly fierce. When arms sales from the United States ceased, China quickly established new ties with Russia to fill their needs (Gill and Kim, 1995). In addition, the European Union (EU) has embraced technology transfers to China, and Airbus (the Boeing equivalent in the EU) is eager to replace Boeing as China's leading aircraft supplier (BXA, 1999: v; Smith and Hamilton, 1995: A14). The reality faced by U.S. business interests is that "one cannot *not* be in China, lest a competitor get a foothold first" (BXA, 1999: 46).

Assessing the Performance of the Exit Model

With the cost of exit exceeding what the United States is willing to bear, China has been successful in extracting demands for technology. The bargaining *power equilibrium* (see figure 4.7) discussed in chapter 3 captures this behavior. The exit model predicts low level conflict, which has been recurrent in the last decade as the United States bristles against the demands being made and continually pushes for market reform and economic access to China. This conflict has not escalated to militarized levels despite frequent clashes over human rights and economic property rights. Given the scope of the demands set forth by the Chinese thus far, the United States has not yet decided to test China to see if rejecting technological access also restricts U.S. access to the Chinese economy or escalates political tensions.

Figure 4.7. China-U.S. Bargaining Power Equilibrium

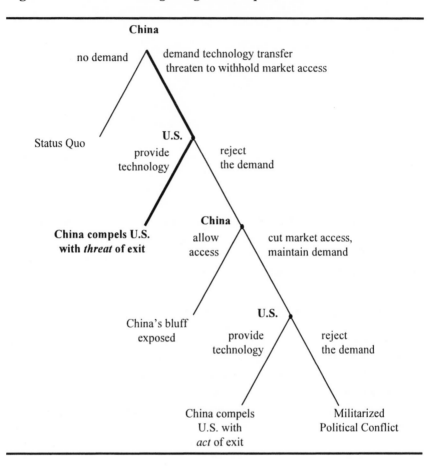

The China-United States example also reveals a shortcoming of the model in that it assumes each state acts as a unitary actor (unified bodies that in this case can represent over a billion people). Beyond the sheer size of each country and the almost certain diversity of preferences within them, this assumption is problematic because the economic ties that link the two states are motivated by sub-state interests. Firms, industries, and consumers are the driving forces behind the increase in economic interaction. In China, this is less true due to the command economy market structure, but within the United States, the internal diversity has polarized its citizens on the issue of how much to sacrifice to maintain market access in China. This assumption is bolstered, however, by the fact that U.S. government bodies such as the Department of Commerce and specifically the Bureau of Export Administration (a division of the Department of Commerce) monitor and approve all contracts between U.S. firms and China that deal with technology transfer (BXA, 1999). Thus, the decision to allow technology transfers remains somewhat centralized in the U.S. administration.

Escalation: Great Britain, Argentina, and War in 1982

The third case in this chapter involves the military conflict between Great Britain and Argentina in 1982. In this case, Great Britain reacted to Argentina's invasion of the Falkland/Malvinas islands with a demand that Argentina remove its troops.[4] Great Britain bolstered this demand with the threat of economic sanctions and the possibility of military conflict. This case provides an interesting perspective because Great Britain managed to alter the market structure associated with the exit costs faced by Argentina by eliciting joint sanctions from the European Economic Community (EEC) (Martin, 1992). Despite these efforts, Argentina rejected Great Britain's demands both before and after sanctions were implemented. Great Britain then escalated the conflict, using military force to reclaim the islands.

In this section, I examine the exit costs faced by Argentina and Great Britain relative to their exit cost thresholds. I define Great Britain as the Challenger, and Argentina as the Target. The demand issued by Great Britain was for Argentina to relinquish its newfound control of the Falklands/Malvinas islands, and the economic exit option involved sanctions that froze Argentine assets in Great Britain and ceased all trade between the two countries. For both states, domestic pressures increased the political value of the islands and in turn drove up the exit cost thresholds such that they exceeded actual exit costs incurred during the sanctions. As both states faced exit costs that were tolerable relative to the endurance thresholds, this case is well informed by the *escalation equilibrium* derived in chapter 3. Before examining these exit costs, however, let us first revisit briefly the events surrounding the Falklands/Malvinas islands conflict. The British demand for Argentina to relinquish control over the islands occurred after Argentina's initial invasion. The timing of this event sequence is complex, and a little historical perspective will help us determine the set of events that are related to the exit model.

Historical Perspective

The acute conflict between Great Britain and Argentina over the Falkland/Malvinas islands began in April of 1982, but the origins of the dispute trace back to the early nineteenth century. These small islands, located 480 miles northwest of Cape Horn in the Atlantic, were first claimed by Argentinia in 1820. British forces replaced the Argentine flag with their own in 1833 and maintained sovereignty of the islands until the dispute escalated in 1982. Throughout nearly two centuries of British rule, Argentina has maintained its claim to the islands. Diplomatic efforts to reclaim the islands began again in earnest in the 1960s as decolonization became popular in the UN, and Argentina repeatedly initiated talks with Great Britain to achieve a peaceful solution to the dispute. These talks occurred as late as February of 1982 (Gamba, 1987).[5]

Argentina changed tactics in March of 1982. Using a commercial scrap metal recovery mission as cover, Argentina made a covert attempt to establish a base on South Georgia Island (a British island proximate to the Falklands/Malvinas). There was precedent for these actions, as Argentina had established a base on the island of South Thule in 1976 and had not met serious resistance from the British. This time, Great Britain resisted and demanded that the Argentinians leave South Georgia. When it became clear that the Argentine presence on the island was not leaving on its own accord, Great Britain dispatched a ship with Marines to ensure that the sovereignty of South Georgia remained intact (Freedman and Gamba-Stonehouse, 1990).

The ruling junta in Argentina, headed by President Galtieri, sent reinforcements to the island in late March in an attempt to head off the British removal of Argentine workers. In addition, Galtieri used this escalating crisis in South Georgia to initiate a forced claim on the Falklands/Malvinas Islands. Galtieri feared that the British reinforcements that were heading into the area were not only intended to remove the Argentine workers from South Georgia, but also to beef up security for the Falklands/Malvinas Islands (Freedman and Gamba-Stonehouse, 1990: 68). The window of opportunity to reclaim the islands was closing quickly, and Argentina sought to take advantage of superior but temporary position. On April 2, Argentinian commando and amphibious forces landed on the Falklands/Malvinas Islands. By the afternoon the invasion was complete. Galtieri's hope was to hold onto the islands long enough to achieve a diplomatic victory in the UN which would bolster their claim that the islands indeed belonged to them.

Argentina, having invaded the islands successfully, hoped that they had reached a stopping point in their dispute with Great Britain over the islands. In order to maintain secrecy in their intentions to occupy the Falklands/Malvinas, they did not threaten Great Britain with the possibility of military force (Freedman and Gamba-Stonehouse, 1990). Argentina sought at this point to maintain a new status quo. It was now up to Great Britain to either accept their loss of the islands or take steps to reclaim them.

It is at this point in the sequence of events that the exit model becomes relevant. Although the chain of events surrounding the Falklands/Malvinas Islands precedes this stage, up to this point no threats of economic exit have accompanied political demands.[6] Great Britain now faced a situation where it could either accept Argentina's claim on the islands or demand that Argentina relinquish control. Using UN Security Council Resolution 502 as a platform, Great Britain issued its demand along with the threat of economic sanctions (Freedman and Gamba-Stonehouse, 1990: 140).[7] Argentina now faced the role of the Target, and could either accept the demands and give up the Falklands/Malvinas, or reject it and stand firm.

Fearing it would lose the ability to negotiate over the islands, Argentina refused to back down. On April 6 the British imposed a ban on imports from Argentina. Four days later the European Economic Community (EEC) joined Great Britain in imposing trade sanctions. Argentina retaliated with sanctions on British and EEC imports (Hufbauer et al., 1990b: 537; Brecher and Wilkenfeld, 1997: 526). Toward the end of April the United States also joined in sanctions against Argentina and declared its support for Great Britain. British troops arrived in the area near the Malvinas/Falklands Islands in late April, but Argentina still would not relinquish the islands (Martin, 1992: 152).

May 1, 1982 marked the beginning of an escalation of the conflict, as British troops initiated force against the Argentine military. Within the week, planes and ships were destroyed on both sides. The death toll surged into the hundreds with Argentina bearing the brunt of the casualties. Economic and diplomatic tools had failed to produce a resolution to the dispute, and the two sides resorted to force to settle the issue. The conflict was short-lived, and Argentina surrendered to the British on June 14. Galtieri resigned as president, and within months the military junta in Argentina fell (Martin, 1992: 152; Brecher and Wilkenfeld, 1997: 526).

Cost-Benefit Analysis

The initial impact of Great Britain's imposition of economic exit was minimal to Argentina in both absolute and proportional trade levels. Great Britain's imports from Argentina in 1980 totaled $271 million. Figure 4.8 shows that in 1980 Argentina's trade with Great Britain represented approximately three percent of Argentina's total trade (Hufbauer et al., 1990b; Barbieri, 2002). Great Britain's ability to recruit the rest of the EEC to join in its economic exit, however, raised the ante by generating a larger presence in the market structure for Argentina. EEC trade with Argentina represented roughly twenty percent of Argentina's total trade, a sizeable improvement over Great Britain's three percent share. To make matters worse, Argentina faced "rapidly deteriorating economic and political conditions" at home (Martin, 1992: 148-54). By the end of April, the United States was on board as well. With the EEC and the United States joining in on sanctions, Great Britain was able to impose a costly economic exit upon Argentina.

These sanctions were costly to the British as well, but for different reasons. Obtaining cooperation from the EEC was no easy task, and Great Britain applied considerable pressure to maintain EEC unity throughout the crisis. Ireland, Belgium, and Italy all expressed reservations against joining in the sanctions, and Martin argues that these nations were only willing to join the EEC to preserve the solidarity of the group and avoid a military conflict (1992). Once military fighting broke out, Great Britain had to concede on two issues in the EEC that were linked to the group's support of the sanctions. Before the crisis, Great Britain had been pursuing a reduction in its contribution to the EEC budget. It was also opposing an increase in supports for farm prices. Both issues were linked by other EEC countries (Ireland, Italy, and West Germany) to the approval and renewal of sanctions against Argentina. Before the crisis was over, Great Britain had lost its fight to block the farm price support increases and yielded almost $400 million in its quest for budget contribution reductions.

Given the costs Great Britain had to pay to maintain cohesive economic sanctions from the EEC, what motivated the British to pursue this demand in the first place? There were less than 2000 British citizens living on the islands. At least until the mid-1960s, the islands were considered a low priority for Great Britain (Gamba, 1987: 88). The invasion of the islands by Argentina and its subsequent reluctance to give them back to Great Britain are similarly puzzling. Argentina did have a historical claim to the islands, but the primary concerns of the military junta headed by Galtieri were to phase out human rights abuses and restore the economy. What motivated the Argentine government to risk stability and economic recovery over these islands? The answer to the motivations for both countries has surprisingly little to do with the islands themselves and much to do with domestic conditions.

At home in England, Margaret Thatcher's Conservative Party was having trouble with popular and electoral support. The value of the issue at stake went far beyond the physical value of the islands. Popular opinion in England was firmly against allowing Argentina to keep the islands. The issue quickly became critical for Thatcher's survival, as "any outcome that looked like a British surrender would almost certainly have led to demands that Thatcher resign" (Martin, 1992: 151). The elevation of the Falkland/Malvinas Islands to such a high priority in British politics was due in large part to the efforts of a small but powerful lobby group in London: the Falkland Islands Pressure Group.

In 1968 the two nations were close to a settlement over the Falkland/Malvinas Islands with a "near-transference of sovereignty to Argentina" (Gamba, 1987: 90). The Falkland Islands Pressure Group, founded in late 1967, began a heated campaign against the negotiations. Their efforts were enough to halt progress in the negotiations, leaving a bitter split between Argentina and Great Britain. The sole purpose of this group has been to prevent any sovereignty concessions by the part of the British to Argentina. This group persists in this goal even today, remaining vigilant throughout regime changes in both countries. Gamba considers the efforts of this lobby group in 1968 as "the single most important milestone in considering the war of 1982" (1987: 93). Most importantly, the Falkland Islands Pressure Group was successful in linking the low priority issue of the islands to important political issues of the day. These linkages inflated the value the British associated with its control of the islands.

Argentina's value of the Falkland/Malvinas Islands was similarly inflated by domestic factors. The economic reforms that had performed remarkably in the late 1970s had turned on the Argentine military government, and the first two years of the 1980s brought high unemployment, interest rates, and a decline in national industry (Gamba, 1987: 75). Galtieri's regime had made significant progress toward ending the human rights abuses for which the military government was infamous, but the government continued to suffer in popular support. As Galtieri instituted austerity packages to try to lower inflation and restore economic credibility to encourage foreign investment, the resulting short-term economic suffering led to sharply declining popular support.

Figure 4.8. Trade between Great Britain and Argentina

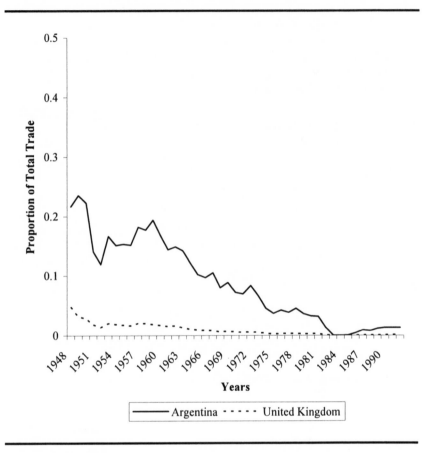

Source: Barbieri, 2002

These same political and economic woes that exacerbated the exit costs that Argentina faced also served to destabilize the regime. Thus, Galtieri gambled that the sovereignty of the Falklands/Malvinas Islands would prove to be a sufficient distraction for his country from their domestic problems. A success on this front would go a long way toward spurring nationalist sentiment and would potentially spark the nation's support for the government, providing Galtieri with much-needed time to ride out the hardships of his tough economic policies until the economy rebounded.

Initially, Galtieri's gamble proved to be successful. Popular discontent and growing labor strikes shifted to rallying support for the troops that had claimed the islands for Argentina. It appeared that Galtieri had bought himself much-needed time to allow his economy to heal. When the UN passed Resolution 502 condemning Argentina's takeover of the islands, the strategy began to unravel. The loss of the islands would mean not only a humiliating defeat for Argentina, but also disaster for Galtieri. He realized that the only way to maintain his newfound popular support would be to stand firm against British demands. Galtieri and the Argentine government placed a very high value on maintaining sovereignty of the Falkland/Malvinas Islands; they now associated keeping the islands with remaining in power.

The relative military capabilities of Argentina and Great Britain appeared to be balanced as the crisis began. While the British possessed an absolute advantage militarily, the problems involved with organizing a military campaign so far from home were significant. Martin relates the conditions that dampened Great Britain's advantage and suggested the probability of success in a military conflict for both states were roughly equal:

> . . . many observers had doubts about Britain's ability to win a military confrontation. Argentina had a logistical advantage, with British forces having to operate 8000 miles from home. Argentine military forces were equipped with advanced, modern armaments, some of them purchased from Britain. In addition, the Argentine forces had the advantage of defending, rather than trying to invade, the islands. (1992: 152)

The costs of such a fight also seemed to favor Argentina. The distance involved for the British sending troops to the islands raised the cost of the mission considerably. This same location enabled Argentina to maneuver its troops easily in place.

Assessing the Performance of the Exit Model

Putting the pieces together, both states faced serious exit costs associated with the sanctions imposed by the British and the EEC. For Great Britain, these costs came not only from the sanctions themselves but also from the concessions it had to make in order to maintain a unified front with the EEC. For Argentina, the costs were exacerbated by Great Britain's ability to garner cooperation from the EEC and the United States. Great Britain's ability to generate market power through this cooperation increased Argentina's costs of exit almost tenfold.

Despite these costs, however, the political value associated with possession of the Falklands/Malvinas Islands by both the Argentine and the British governments dominated the equation. The survival of both governments quickly became linked to the issue of who controlled the islands, and this linkage drove up their exit cost thresholds. The probability of winning an escalated conflict was too balanced to deter either side, and even the costs of fighting were dwarfed by this inflated sense of importance over the islands.

The result was a set of exit cost thresholds that exceeded the actual exit costs each state faced. The *escalation* equilibrium predicts that when both states face exit costs that are endurable, the economic interdependence will fail to constrain the states from using conflict to settle their dispute. Dillon concludes that the decision to fight was a clear choice for both states:

> . . . if decision makers are to control the dynamics of crisis and retain any prospect of preserving peace . . . both sides must fear war and the loss of control over the situation more than they do the loss of whatever is at stake in their confrontation. Clearly neither Argentina nor the United Kingdom subscribed to this condition. The leadership of both countries, backed by popular support, was prepared to risk the gamble of a military contest rather than accept the political and national humiliation of an unsatisfactory compromise. (1989: 91-92)

Figure 4.9 shows the progression of the game as applied to this case, and the escalation equilibrium path was followed without deviation. Argentina rejected the UK's demand both before and after the UK imposed economic sanctions, and the result was a military conflict that claimed almost a thousand casualties (Brecher and Wilkenfeld, 1997: 526).

As with the other cases, the Great Britain-Argentina conflict over the Falklands/Malvinas Islands is not a perfect fit for the exit model. In particular, the model does not account for a very important third player in the crisis: the United States. Initially on the fence because both Argentina and Great Britain were U.S. allies, the United States sided with the British in late April of 1982. Alexander Haig, U.S. Secretary of State at the time, sought to mediate the conflict to reach a compromise settlement and avoid escalation, but when the fighting broke out the U.S. support of the British solidified (Gamba, 1987). The case also demonstrates the difficulty in determining both the probability of conflict success and the cost of fighting for either state. In the end, the costs of fighting for Argentina included the loss of 700 lives (250 for the British), and it is a strain to assume that either state could have predicted these costs before the conflict erupted (Brecher and Wilkenfeld, 1997: 526).

Figure 4.9. Great Britain-Argentina Escalation Equilibrium

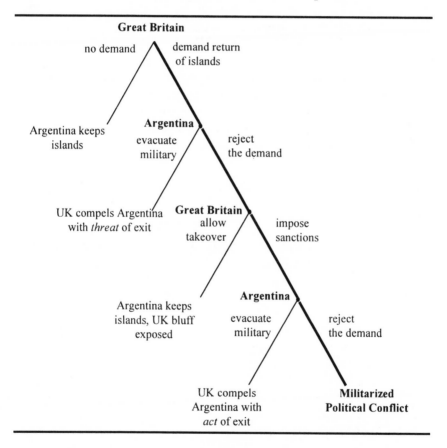

Conclusion

These cases have demonstrated that the abstract exit model developed and analyzed in chapter 3 does indeed inform the study of economic interdependence and political conflict. The cases flesh out the abstract model and help us gain an intuitive and empirical sense of the strategic interaction driving the model. The diversity across the cases shows how the exit model captures complex interstate behavior, and drives home the point that the relationship between economic interdependence and political conflict is not at all straightforward.

The empirical analysis in this chapter also reveals some weaknesses in the exit model. The case of the United States and South Africa highlighted the problem of determining when a threat of economic exit is at hand (as opposed to minor economic sanctions), as well as the inability of the model to capture partial acceptance by the Target state. The China–United States case called the unitary actor assumption into question and revealed one of the most difficult challenges to the study of international economics and politics together. Politics is motivated at the state level, but economics is often motivated at a sub-state level. Finally, the Great Britain–Argentina case demonstrated the difficulty in assuming states can have a priori knowledge about the costs and outcomes of war.

These shortcomings of the exit model, however, can be overcome in future research. All of the problematic assumptions of the model identified here can be relaxed to provide a more general model. The demand can be modeled as an endogenous choice for the Challenger, and the Target's option of accept-reject can be transformed into a policy space between these two extreme options. The preferences of the states can be modeled as functions of domestic politics, which in turn can generate situations of incomplete information in the model with respect to exit costs or exit cost thresholds. These are all priorities of future research.

Despite these shortcomings, the basic exit model succeeds in providing an explicit theory of how economic interdependence can negatively affect conflict (high and low levels), positively affect low-level conflict, or fail to influence states away from the decision to use force. The model not only predicts this broad range of influence; it more importantly provides us with enough information to know when to expect each particular outcome. The cases analyzed here illustrate this explanatory power and provide empirical evidence suggesting that the exit model can be a useful tool for scholars and policy makers. In the next chapter, I provide a very different kind of empirical assessment of the exit model. Whereas this chapter focused on three historical cases that illustrated the explanatory power of the exit model, in chapter 5 I derive more abstract but empirically testable hypotheses from the exit model. I then test these hypotheses using a multivariate, cross-sectional approach. Together, these two chapters provide a balanced empirical assessment of the exit model.

Notes

1. Indeed, the three cases show that not all sanctions represent exit, and not all exit options are sanctions.

2. See *The Report of the Study Commission on US Policy Toward Southern Africa* (SCUSPTSA1981: 310).

3. Chromium reserves are in Kazakhstan, manganese reserves are in the Ukraine, and platinum can be found in Russia.

4. The islands are referred to as the Falklands by the British and the Malvinas by the Argentinians. The UN has resolved the issue by labeling them the Falkland/Malvinas Islands.

5. For more on the history of the Falklands/Malvinas Islands and their role in British-Argentine relations, see Dillon (1989), Freedman and Gamba-Stonehouse (1990), and Gamba (1987).

6. In any case, because the analysis of the model in the last chapter produces equilibria that are subgame perfect, the game does not have to represent the entirety of the events which transpired between Great Britain and Argentina. In effect, the game tree is really a "branch" of a much larger, unspecified game. In order to investigate the rationality and strategy of Argentina's invasion of the Falklands/Malvinas Islands (or, for that matter, the British invasion in the 1830s), we would need to extend the game to reflect this broader puzzle. As I am chiefly concerned here with the effect of economic exit as a bargaining tool, employing the exit model in this situation where the threat of exit first emerges is optimal for this analysis.

7. Galtieri's anticipation of diplomatic support in the UN proved to be incorrect. The resolution condemned the invasion and called for unilateral withdrawal of Argentine troops.

5

An Empirical Test of the Exit Model

This chapter complements the empirical investigation of the exit model in chapter 4 using a quantitative approach to test implications of the exit model. Whereas chapter 4 illustrated the exit model's ability to capture the strategic behavior of nations engaged in political and economic relationships, this chapter assesses the model's empirical performance in a more systematic fashion. Specifically, I test the central analytical result of the exit model: economic interdependence (in which at least one state faces exit costs that exceed its threshold) decreases the likelihood of escalated conflict, but increases the likelihood of low-level conflict. I also examine the hypothesis that it is the Target's exit cost levels that trigger low-level conflict, while high-level conflict is inhibited by the presence of high exit costs for either state. Finally, I assess the role of capability and the likelihood of success in high-level conflict.

The hypotheses developed below are derived directly from the equilibrium analysis of the exit model. Despite this direct link, however, the analysis in this chapter does not match the qualitative analysis in chapter 4 in terms of matching empirical content to the strategic interaction of the model. The approach taken here demands abstraction that provides greater confidence in the external validity of the results at the expense of a rich representation of the model and its predictions. Economic interdependence becomes the causal variable and is operationalized by measuring exit costs via the interaction of bilateral price elasticities, trade, and GDP (Marquez, 1990; Barbieri, 1995; Oneal and Russett, 1997). Political conflict, the phenomena to be explained, is broken down into status quo (no conflict) and low- and high-level conflict and operationalized using the WEIS event data set (Goldstein, 1992). The statistical analysis provides empirical support for the exit model via the hypotheses derived from the formal analysis in chapter 3.

Hypotheses: Deriving Implications from the Exit Model

Two basic hypotheses emerge regarding the causal impact of economic interdependence upon political conflict. The first involves the ability of the Challenger to use the exit costs of the Target as predicted in the bargaining power equilibrium. The second hypothesis sets forth the proposition that economic interdependence creates a more efficient arena within which issues and disputes are addressed, thereby reducing the occurrence of higher degrees of conflict. A third hypothesis is derived from the comparative static analysis of the game, and it suggests that the probability of success in high-level conflict plays an important role in determining the impact of economic interdependence on the occurrence of political conflict at all levels.

Exit Costs, Thresholds, and Political Conflict

The analysis of the exit model focuses on the relationship between exit costs and exit cost thresholds for both players. Four possible combinations of the exit cost and exit cost threshold parameters produce three equilibrium paths, each with a unique predicted outcome of the game. Table 5.1 summarizes these variable combinations and the associated outcomes. Note that the exit cost to exit cost threshold relationships must be examined for both states in the game in order to determine the predicted outcome, except for the bargaining power equilibrium. For this equilibrium (case two), it is only the Target's exit cost and cost threshold that determines the prediction of the low-level conflict outcome.

Table 5.1. Exit Costs and Equilibrium Behavior

Equilibrium	Exit Cost—Threshold Relationship	Predicted Outcome
Case One: Constraint	$e_{Ch} > e_{Ch}^*,$ $e_T < e_T^*$	Status Quo
Case Two: Bargaining Power	$e_T > e_T^*, e_{Ch} > e_{Ch}^*$ or $e_T > e_T^*, e_{Ch} < e_{Ch}^*$	Low-level Conflict
Case Three: Escalation	$e_{Ch} < e_{Ch}^*,$ $e_T < e_T^*$	High-level Conflict

(*) denotes threshold vs. actual exit costs

Exit Costs and Low-level Conflict

The relationships between these variables and the outcomes that specify the occurrence of low- or high-level conflict are translated here into testable hypotheses. The first task is to differentiate between the economic conditions that lead to status quo versus low-conflict behavior. The constraint equilibrium suggests that status quo behavior can be expected when the Challenger faces exit costs that exceed its threshold *and* the Target faces exit costs that are less than its threshold ($e_{Ch} > e_{Ch}^*$ and $e_T < e_T^*$). The bargaining power equilibrium, on the other hand, states that low-level conflict occurs when the Target faces exit costs that exceed the Target's threshold ($e_T > e_T^*$), regardless of the Challenger's economic situation. The difference between the status quo and low-level conflict outcomes lies in the Target's exit costs vis-à-vis its exit cost threshold. This relationship between low-level conflict and the exit costs and threshold of the Target state can be restated in the following hypothesis:

> H1:   *If exit costs for the Target exceed the Target's exit cost threshold, then low-level conflict will be present. This holds even if the exit costs for the Challenger exceed its exit cost threshold.*

This hypothesis presents problems for large-n research, however, because it requires the researcher to know the exit cost threshold level of the Target. This threshold level is a function of the value the Target associates with the issue at stake in a dispute with a Challenger state, as well as the costs of high-level conflict and the likelihood of winning such a conflict. Quantifying the value of the demand for either state on a large-n basis is not possible, which in turn makes the exit cost thresholds unobservable.

A solution to this problem is to make some abstract assumptions about the likelihood of where an exit cost threshold lies on the range of possible values (Crescenzi, 1999). Figure 5.1 graphically shows how the exit cost threshold splits the range of possible exit costs into two one-dimensional spaces. The first range is specified by the set of possible exit costs that are less than the threshold. Two equilibria can occur when a target's exit costs fall in this range: the status quo equilibrium (case one) and the escalation equilibrium (case three). The second range is defined by the set of exit costs that exceed the target's threshold. This bargaining power equilibrium (case three) emerges when the target's exit costs fall in this second range. Assuming that the exit cost threshold is unknown *but fixed*, and that the possible values for this threshold are uniformly distributed, it follows that higher levels of exit costs are more likely to be in this second range than lower levels of exit costs.

These assumptions allow me to restate the first hypothesis into a crude but testable alternative. If higher exit costs for the target increase the likelihood of observing the bargaining power equilibrium, then we should also expect to observe the low-level conflict associated with this equilibrium. This suggests the following alternative to H1:

> *H1a:*   *Higher exit costs for the Target increase the likelihood that these costs exceed the cost threshold. Therefore, higher Target exit costs increase the likelihood that low-level conflict will occur.*

This alternate hypothesis recasts the proposed relationship between exit costs and low-level conflict in a probabilistic language, and testing this hypothesis does not require information about the exit cost threshold.

Figure 5.1. Exit Costs and Threshold for the Target

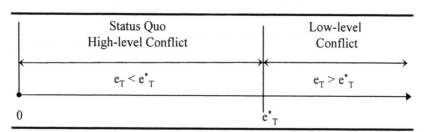

A second hypothesis also derives from the bargaining power equilibrium. One of the counterintuitive results of the exit model is that the Challenger's exit costs are irrelevant in this equilibrium. The exit cost to threshold relationships in table 5.1 are only relevant for the Target. Even a Challenger who faces exit costs that exceed its own threshold can use the economic relationship to extract demands from the Target. This logic leads to the following hypothesis:

> *H1b:* *Higher Challenger exit costs will not increase the likelihood of low-level conflict.*

This hypothesis suggests that information is needed regarding the direction of events within a dyad (events initiated by the Challenger versus initiated by the Target).

Exit Costs and High-level Conflict

The exit costs to cost-threshold relationships for the Challenger and Target in the escalation equilibrium stipulate the conditions in which economic interdependence is ineffective in reducing the occurrence of high levels of conflict. Table 5.1 shows that *both* states have to face exit costs that are lower than their respective thresholds ($e_{Ch} < e_{Ch}^*$ and $e_T < e_T^*$). This joint condition leads to the next hypothesis:

> *H2:* *If exit costs for either the Challenger or the Target exceed their exit cost thresholds, then the occurrence of escalated conflict is constrained by economic interdependence.*

This hypothesis generates the same problems as H1, and I use the same logic to translate H2 into the following two alternative hypotheses:

> *H2a:*   *Higher exit costs for the Target decrease the*
>   *likelihood of high levels of conflict.*
>
> *H2b:*   *Higher exit costs for the Challenger also de-*
>   *crease the likelihood of high-level conflict.*

Since high exit costs for either state can decrease the incidence of high-level conflict, directionality of events within the dyad is not important for these hypotheses.

Controlling for the Probability of Success

Thus far, the focus has been on real exit costs vs. exit cost thresholds. An alternative tool for deriving hypotheses from game-theoretic models is the use of comparative statics to see how the costs and benefits involved in the moves of the game influence the exit cost thresholds. From chapter 3 we know that the thresholds for the Challenger and Target are:

$$e_{Ch}^* = p(v_{Ch}) - c_{Ch} \qquad\qquad (3.3)$$

$$e_T^* = (1-p)(v_T) - c_T . \qquad\qquad (3.4)$$

The factors that determine the thresholds, e_{CH}^* and e_T^*, are the value of the issue at stake (v_{Ch} and v_T), the cost of fighting (c_{Ch} and c_T), and the probability that the Challenger would be successful in the event of escalated conflict (p). Based on these threshold functions, I focus on how each factor affects the threshold level, holding all other factors constant.

Table 5.2 presents the results of this analysis. For both states, the value of the issue at stake drives up their respective thresholds. That is, as the value of the issue goes up, so does a state's tolerance for the costs of economic exit, making economic statecraft less effective. Thus, issues involving territory, national security, or economic stability are likely to generate higher thresholds than more minor issues such as treaty enforcement, domestic policy disagreements (e.g., human rights or labor policy), or tariff level disputes.

The cost of fighting has the opposite effect. As this cost increases for either state, their respective thresholds decrease regardless of the likelihood of success in the conflict. This suggests that a potential conflict involving ground troops, extended deployments and high casualties will generate lower exit cost thresholds than a potential conflict requiring only air and sea campaigns or a short duration with low casualty expectations.[1]

Table 5.2. Parametric Relationships

Relationship	Description
$v_{Ch} \uparrow \Rightarrow e^*_{Ch} \uparrow$	As the value of the demand increases, the Challenger is willing to bear higher costs of economic exit to pursue this demand.
$p \uparrow \Rightarrow e^*_{Ch} \uparrow$	As the likelihood that the Challenger will win an escalated conflict increases, it is willing to bear higher costs of economic exit to pursue a political demand.
$c_{Ch} \uparrow \Rightarrow e^*_{Ch} \downarrow$	As the cost of engaging in an escalated conflict increases, the Challenger's threshold of economic cost of exit decreases.
$V_T \uparrow \Rightarrow e^*_T \uparrow$	As the value of the demand increases, the Target is willing to bear higher costs of exit to avoid giving in to the Challenger's demands.
$p \uparrow \Rightarrow e^*_T \downarrow$	As the likelihood that the Challenger will win an escalated conflict increases, the Target's threshold of economic cost of exit decreases.
$c_T \uparrow \Rightarrow e^*_T \downarrow$	As the cost of engaging in an escalated conflict increases, the Target's threshold of economic exit cost of exit decreases.

The third factor, the probability of success for the Challenger, has opposite effects for Challenger and Target. An increase in this probability drives up the Challenger's exit cost threshold, but decreases the threshold of the Target. If this probability is taken to be an indication of relative power, then power disparity in favor of the Challenger makes the Challenger more willing to endure higher exit costs, but weakens the ability of the Target to endure the costs of exit.

Of the three factors involved in this comparative statics analysis, only one factor, the probability of success for the Challenger, lends itself to the large-n analysis of this work. The other factors, issue value and cost of conflict, require detailed information that is currently unavailable for quantitative research. As such, I focus here only on the Challenger's likelihood of winning the potential escalated conflict. The comparative static results in table 5.2 regarding this factor indicate that an increase in the likelihood that the Challenger wins the high-level conflict results in an increase for the Challenger's exit threshold and a decrease for the threshold of the Target. This linkage can be restated as the following hypothesis:

> *H3:*   *An increase in the likelihood that the Challenger will defeat the Target in an escalated conflict raises the Challenger's threshold and drops the threshold of the Target. This in turn decreases the likelihood that the Challenger's exit costs exceed its threshold, and increases the likelihood that the exit costs of the Target exceed its threshold.*

As with the earlier hypotheses, the inability of the researcher to observe actual exit cost thresholds leads to the following alternatives:

> *H3a:*   *An increase in the likelihood that the Challenger will defeat the Target decreases the likelihood of high-level conflict.*

> *H3b:*   *An increase in the likelihood that the Challenger will defeat the Target increases the likelihood of low-level conflict.*

The inclusion of this probability factor in the analysis below serves two purposes. First, it allows us to examine this third set of hypotheses regarding the impact of the probability of high-level conflict success on the incidence of low- and high-level conflict. Second, the impact of this factor on the exit cost thresholds suggests that its inclusion in the analysis serves as a control in the investigation of the other hypotheses. Specifically, the value of p influences the level of the exit cost threshold. If high values of p drive up the threshold of the Challenger and drive down the threshold of the Target, this affects the likelihood that the actual exit costs of both states fall above or below these thresholds (see figure 5.1 and the discussion above). Because the alternative hypotheses rely on the assumed probability distribution of the thresholds, the effect of p in turn influences the ability of hypotheses 1a, 1b, 2a, and 2b to accurately reflect the logic of hypotheses 1 and 2. Thus, the inclusion of the probability of conflict success is an important addition to the analysis of economic interdependence and political conflict.

With these three sets of hypotheses established, the next section lays out the research design of the analysis. I operationalize the concepts of economic interdependence, political conflict, and the probability of success in high-level conflict, followed by data selection and statistical methodology.

Research Design

Economic Interdependence: Trade, Inelasticity, and Exit Costs

The challenge here is to develop a valid measure of exit costs and thus interdependence while maintaining the systematic and general approach of a large-n analysis. To this end I interact bilateral price elasticity data (Marquez, 1990) with trade activity data (Barbieri, 1995; Oneal and Russett, 1997) in a joint representation of market structure and intensity of potential economic exit costs. In chapter 2, I define these exit costs using two factors: market structure and asset specificity. Market structure refers to the degree to which one state can turn to other suppliers or consumers in the global market for goods, services, and market access withheld by another state imposing economic exit. Asset specificity is concerned with the internal response to economic exit, and thus refers to a state's ability to find substitutes for suspended goods, services, and market access.

Both dimensions deal with the ability of states to adapt and react to economic change. Measuring these factors of exit costs has proved to be difficult, with the majority of empirical work appearing in the form of single country case studies (see Alston et al., 1996; Williamson, 1996). In order to establish a generalizable measure of a state's ability to adapt to economic change, I operationalize exit costs using the following two pieces of information: price inelasticity and intensity of economic exchange.

The first piece involves measuring market structure and asset specificity using the inelasticity of import prices. Price elasticities measure the sensitivity of a nation to a change in the price of imports using the following logic (Landsburg, 1995):

$$Price\ Elasticity = \frac{Percentage\ Change\ in\ Quanitity\ of\ Imports}{Percentage\ Change\ in\ Price\ of\ Imports}. \qquad (5.1)$$

Price elasticity is a measure of a state's ability to adjust its demand for imports given a change in import prices. A state that is able to curb its demand for imports when prices rise and expand its demand for these imports when prices fall has an elastic demand for the imports. For example, in the late 1990s Japan experienced an economic recession. The resulting income effect led to a relative price increase for apples imported from the U.S. state of Washington.[2] Consumption of the apples dropped considerably, much to the chagrin of the growers in Washington. Japan's demand for these apples is elastic precisely because it can tailor its consumption of the good to match price changes. At the other end of the spectrum, a state that cannot alter the amount of imports it needs given an increase or decrease in prices has an inelastic demand. Oil imports exemplify goods that tend to be inelastic. In essence, import price elasticities are a measure of the fungibility of a state's demand for imported goods and services.

Price elasticities are often discussed at the goods level, and it is natural to expect that import price elasticities will vary across goods imported from any given state. This is problematic for the study of interstate conflict because the behavior I wish to explain takes place at the dyadic level of analysis (the interaction *between* two states). Marquez (1990) has estimated bilateral import price elasticities that are aggregated to the dyad level, providing information regarding one state's elasticity for the aggregation of all imports from another state. The resulting elasticity estimates allow the extraction of information on one state's market relationship with another, as state level elasticities reflect a state's ability to react to economic change initiated by another state. In addition to being bilateral and aggregated at the state level, the elasticity scores are directional, such that Germany's elasticity score for imports from France is not necessarily the same as France's score for German imports.

Because demand elasticities reflect the slope of the demand curve, they are always negative or zero. A score of zero indicates perfect inelasticity, and larger negative scores reflect increased elasticity. For the purposes of this study, I have adjusted these scores such that positive scores reflect *inelasticity* and a score of zero indicates the most elastic score in the data set. This is done simply by adding the absolute value of the most elastic score to all the estimates in the data set, and I label this indicator *Inelasticity$_{ij}$*, such that *Inelasticity$_{ij}$* is state I's price inelasticity of imports from state J.

The Marquez data is significantly constrained in terms of spatial and temporal scope. He uses import data from the *Direction of Trade* data set published by the International Monetary Fund (1993). The countries included in his study are Canada, Germany, Japan, the United Kingdom, and the United States. He also includes aggregate group estimates for the rest of the OECD countries (which I assume here to be Italy and France), as well as LDC and OPEC countries. I disaggregate the "rest of the OECD" group into Italy and France, but exclude the other groupings because there are too many states included in each group to obtain useful information.[3] Data from 1973 to 1984 is used to compute the elasticity scores, but the scores themselves are cross-sectional and do not vary over time. Marquez tests these estimates for temporal stability and finds that the aggregate price elasticity scores do not vary during the 1973-84 period.

While the Marquez elasticity data measures the adaptability of states to changes in imports from other states, it is also important to assess the degree to which a state needs to implement these changes. That is, I require a measure of how intense the economic relationship is relative to each state's economy and trade portfolio in the global market. This information is important because the degree to which one state involves another in its economy provides additional information about how costly it would be for the first state to endure an exit from this economic relationship. Just as a trade relationship can represent a large portion of a state's economy but still not be costly if this trade is elastic, the same relationship can be inelastic but still not be costly if this trade represents only a small portion of its economy or total global trade.

To capture this concept of the degree of trade relative to a state's total trade or economy, I include in this study two measures of trade intensity. The first measures the amount of imports and exports between two states relative to each state's total trade. This measure was first introduced by Barbieri (1995) and labeled *TradeShare*. The *TradeShare* indicator is dyadic and directional, such that

$$TradeShare_{ij} = \frac{DyadicTrade_{ij}}{TotalTrade_{i}}, \tag{5.2}$$

where *DyadicTrade$_{ij}$* is the total imports and exports between states I and J.

This directionality allows me to assess the *TradeShare* levels for both the Challenger and the Target. Similarly, the second indicator of this degree of economic interaction represents the total imports and exports, this time normalized by state I's Gross Domestic Product (Oneal and Russett, 1997):

$$TradeGDP_{ij} = \frac{DyadicTrade_{ij}}{GDP_i}. \tag{5.3}$$

Currently there is considerable debate regarding which operationalization of this trade intensity is the more valid measure, so I have chosen here to use both measures alternatively in the following analysis. The Barbieri measure captures the degree to which state I relies on state J for imports relative to all of I's import needs. The Oneal and Russett $TradeGDP_{ij}$ measure, on the other hand, captures the intensity of imports from state J relative to I's domestic economy. The measures capture slightly different information, and thus it will be useful to employ them both. Logic and some diagnostic regression analyses suggest that the two indicators are also quite related, so only one indicator will be used at a time in each statistical model below.

The trade data for both indicators are obtained from Barbieri's International Trade data set (Barbieri 2002). GDP data are obtained from the Penn World Tables (Mark 5.6) (Heston and Summers 1991, 1994). The trade and GDP data are averaged from 1966 to 1992 into one cross-sectional value for each directed dyad in order to match the cross sectional structure of the Marquez elasticity data.[4] Case selection is also limited to the spatial set determined by the elasticity data. Such limitations have inspired researchers to eschew elasticity data in favor of increased generality and spatiotemporal domains (Barbieri, 1995), but I argue that the concept of economic interdependence cannot be validly operationalized using trade scores alone.

Using both the elasticity data and the two tradeshare measures, I define exit costs for state I with respect to state J as:

$$Exit\ Costs\ (TotTrade)_{ij} = TradeShare_{ij} * Inelasticity_{ij}$$
$$Exit\ Costs\ (GDP)_{ij} = TradeGDP_{ij} * Inelasticity_{ij} \tag{5.4}$$

These two variables represent the economic interdependence in the dyadic relationship. They are dyadic and directional. For example, the variable $Exit\ Costs\ (GDP)_{ij}$ reads as "the exit costs for state I with respect to its relationship with state J."

The use of import price elasticity and trade data provides a useful but imperfect operationalization of exit costs. It is useful because the inelasticity dimension captures most of the market structure information needed to identify interdependence. The inelasticity data measure the degree to which a state is unable to reduce demand or find alternate sources of imports from another state. In addition, the proportional trade dimension approximates the intensity of the trade relationship. The measure is imperfect, however, because it does not account for third party interdependence. Nevertheless, it is a significant improvement over existing measures. Situations of high levels of economic activity characterized by high elasticity for both states are not characterized as interdependent.

The Dependent Variable: Political Conflict

The predictions that emerge from the exit model suggest that political behavior between states should be organized into three categories: status quo behavior, low-level conflict, and high-level conflict. The conflict variable should also reflect directionality within the dyad (behavior is viewed as action by a Challenger toward a Target). Issues of data availability and performance with respect to content validity are also addressed here. The first task, however, is to specify the difference between status quo behavior and low-level conflict and low- versus high-level conflict.

As the exit model is a story about the presence or absence of conflict, it does not touch on cooperation between states. I choose here to incorporate cooperation into the category of status quo behavior. In addition to cooperative behavior, the status quo category includes neutral interaction. Status quo behavior can even include mildly conflictual interaction, with the important proviso that action or threats do not characterize this interaction. For example, if state I expresses its concern or disagreement with state J's domestic policy, it is categorized as status quo behavior. If, however, state I expresses its concern and issues a demand of action associated with this concern, then the behavior exceeds the status quo category and is considered low-level conflict.

Low-level conflict is defined here as behavior involving non-military threats, demands, and actions against another state. There must be a clear attempt to change the status quo, not just state one's disagreement. This activity could include the threat or imposition of economic sanctions or other forms of exit, halting of negotiations, and breaking agreements. The character of this type of conflict is that it is employed by a state in an attempt to change some dimension of its political or economic relationship with another state, but there is no indication that the revisionist state seeks to use military tools to achieve its goals. Political conflict that includes the threat or use of military force qualifies as high-level conflict.

I define high-level conflict as the use of military tools and threats against another state. This includes threats where force is specified, meaning troop movement and displays of possible force, as well as the use of force. The general rule applied is that the state initiating this behavior is willingly using the military arena to address an issue or dispute it has with a Target state. There is not only a desire by the Challenger to change the status quo, but also a willingness to use military force or the threat of force to achieve this change.

The standard data set employed to represent political conflict variables in quantitative studies of international conflict is the Militarized Interstate Dispute (MID) data set (Jones et al., 1996). Two problems regarding this data, however, make the use of the MID a poor choice for this study. First, the political conflict measure requires information regarding low-level as well as high-level conflict. As its name suggests, the MID data is concerned only with the threat or use of militarized force, and thus captures only the presence or absence of high-level conflict. The second problem relates to the set of cases covered by the elasticity data discussed earlier. All seven of the countries included in the Marquez elasticity data set are democratic states. One of the most heavily examined and exalted stylized facts in international relations is that democracies do not fight one another. An examination of the MID data for this set of countries reveals that the only militarized disputes recorded were between the United States and Canada, events of dubious veracity. As there are virtually no militarized disputes occurring within the spatiotemporal domain of the elasticity data, the use of the MID data set for the political conflict variable cannot be supported.

Instead, I employ the World Events Interaction Survey (WEIS) data, developed by McClelland in 1971 (Goldstein, 1992). This data was originally conceived as categorical data, sixty-one different kinds of events representing the scope of information captured. Each event is coded directionally, with an actor initiating the event against a Target. I assume here that the terms "actor" and "Challenger" are synonymous. Table 5.3 shows how I have recoded these sixty-one events into the three broader categories using the criteria discussed above.[5] This recategorization results in significant information loss, but the relevant qualities of these events with respect to this study are maintained.

A more serious problem is the information loss relating to the temporal aggregation of the data into one cross-sectional observation. In order to match the format of the Marquez elasticity data, the WEIS event data is collapsed from its daily (at least hypothetically) coding to one observation for the entire temporal period of 1966 to 1992. Following the logic of the MID data set, I extract the highest level of conflict during this period.[6] The loss of information from this temporal aggregation ranges from minor to extensive. Some dyads such as Canada-Germany are represented in the WEIS data set in only five *days* during this twenty-seven-year period. Their spotty presence in the data suggests that less drastic aggregations such as yearly data would lead to the opposite problem of not enough information. Other dyads such as the United States and Japan, however, contain over seven hundred observations over the twenty-seven-year period, and focusing only on the most conflictual level of conflict leads to a stark reduction in the available information. Even yearly aggregation in these high-profile dyads, however, can truncate over fifty observations into one.

Nonetheless, this aggregation does have advantages. First, it places the forty directed dyads in the study on equal footing in the data set in that each is represented by one observation. This eliminates a previous bias toward the dyads containing high-profile states (especially the United States). Second, the content validity of the measure is maintained because information can still be extracted regarding the occurrence of low- and high-level conflict.

Table 5.3. WEIS Events Categorized

Status Quo		Low-level Conflict
Extend military assistance	Offer proposal	Halt negotiation
Extend economic aid; give, buy, sell, loan, borrow	Entreat; plead; appeal to; beg	Turn down proposal; reject protest, demand, threat
Make substantive agreement	Meet with; send note	Refuse, oppose; refuse to allow
Give other assistance	Yield position; retreat; evacuate	Reduce routine international activity; recall officials
Grant privilege; diplomatic recognition, de facto relations	Surrender, yield to order, submit to arrest	Detain or arrest person(s)
Promise material support	Ask for information	Threat without specific negative sanction stated
Promise own policy support	Explain or state policy; state future position	Issue order or command, insist, demand compliance
Promise other future support	Request action; call for	Expel organization or group
Endorse other's policy or position; give verbal support	Explicit decline to comment	Order person or personnel out of country
Praise, hail, applaud, extend condolences	Urge or suggest action or policy	Nonmilitary demonstration, walk out on
Ask for material assistance	Comment on situation	Reduce or cut off aid or assistance; act to punish/deprive
Ask for policy assistance	Deny an accusation	Threat with specific negative non-military sanction
Agree to future action or procedure, to meet, or to negotiate	Deny an attributed policy, action, role, or position	Ultimatum, threat with negative sanction and time limit

Status Quo		High-level Conflict
Suspend sanctions, end punishment, call truce	Grant asylum	Threat with force specified
Receive visit, host	Make complaint (not formal)	Break diplomatic relations
Assure, reassure	Cancel or postpone planned event	Armed force mobilization, exercise, display; military buildup
Give state invitation		Noninjury destructive action
Admit wrongdoing, apologize, retract statement	Charge; criticize; blame; disapprove	Nonmilitary destruction/injury
Release and/or return persons or property	Issue formal complaint or protest	Seize position or possessions
Visit; go to	Give warning	Military attack; clash; assault
Express regret; apologize	Denounce; denigrate; abuse	

The most serious problem plaguing the content validity of the political conflict variable is one that is driven by the case rather than the source of data. The case selection restrictions resulting from the use of available elasticity data excludes any dyads that have encountered the most extreme form of political conflict: interstate war. This restriction limits the validity of this study such that I cannot make conclusions about the impact of economic interdependence on war. This limitation highlights the tradeoff between obtaining valid measures of economic interdependence and obtaining valid measures of political conflict (see Barbieri, 1995). In this study, the benefits of employing the elasticity data to generate exit cost data combined with the ability to observe low-level as well as high-level conflict outweigh the costs outlined above. An important avenue of future research, however, is to extend the elasticity data such that case selection issues do not truncate the political conflict variable in this fashion.

Relative Capability: Operationalizing the Probability of High-level Conflict Success

To measure the probability of success in the event of high-level conflict, I use the composite indicator of national capabilities (CINC) developed by Singer, Bremer, and Stuckey (1972). This indicator has been employed to represent power in a more general sense (Kadera, 1995). The measure provides information pertaining to a state's capabilities along six dimensions: iron/steel production, urban population base, total population, total military expenditures, total military personnel, and the total amount of energy production. Each dimension is measured as the state's proportion of the total resources available in the interstate system. The six proportions are then averaged to provide one national capability score for each state relative to the rest of the states in the system.[1] As such, the measure ranges from zero (no capability) to one (total capability).

The next step is to transform this state-level score into dyadic information. I use Oneal and Russett's (1997) specification of relative capabilities to transform the data. Oneal and Russett simply divide the less powerful state's CINC score by the more powerful state's score. Rather than organizing the relative scores by larger and smaller states, I choose to divide the Challenger's CINC score by the Target's CINC score. When the resulting relative CINC score is less than one, the Target is considered more powerful than the Challenger. Scores greater than one indicate that the Challenger is more powerful than the Target.

Methodology

The dichotomous dependent variables, Low-level conflict and High-level conflict, suggest that using an ordinary least squares (OLS) method to estimate the relationship between the dependent and independent variables is inappropriate (King, 1989; Liao, 1994). Instead, I use logistic regression. This is a technique designed to estimate relationships between variables when the dependent variable is discrete. This approach is also consistent with current estimation techniques in the study of trade and conflict (Barbieri, 1996; Oneal and Russett, 1997).

The estimated logit models will be assessed in two ways. The primary goal of the analysis is to obtain information regarding the direction and statistical significance of the parameter estimates for the economic variables with respect to the political conflict dependent variables. This information is used to assess the hypotheses laid out above. In addition, I am interested in the performance of the logit models that include the economic independent variables relative to the null model (constant only). I am also interested in whether the performance of the logit models containing the Capability Ratio control variable is superior to that of the logit models without this control.

To conduct this comparison between logit models, one model must be "nested" within the other such that the nested model is restricted so that all of its variables are also present in the larger model, but the reverse is not true. Thus, the null model (constant only) is nested in all the other models, and the models without control variables are nested within their counterparts that contain the Capability Ratio control variable (Long, 1997). I use the likelihood ratio test (King, 1989; Liao, 1994) to assess the relative goodness of fit of these models.[8]

Analysis

Each logit model is examined in two stages. The first stage addresses a basic argument in one of the first four hypotheses (H1a, 1b, 2a, 2b), and the second stage reexamines this argument with the addition of the Capability Ratio control variable (H3a or 3b). Both stages are repeated for each of the two trade variable specifications (total trade and GDP), resulting in four equation estimations for each model. Table 5.4 summarizes the variables employed in the analyses below, using the subscripts c and t to represent the Challenger and Target.

Table 5.4. Variable Definitions

Variables	Description
High-level conflict$_{ct}$	Pool of event types initiated by Challenger against Target. Dummy variable: scored 1 for high-level conflict as most conflictual event, 0 otherwise. Source: WEIS
Low-level conflict$_{ct}$	Pool of event types initiated by Challenger against Target. Dummy variable: scored 1 for low-level conflict as most conflictual event, 0 otherwise. Source: WEIS
Status Quo$_{ct}$	Pool of event types initiated by Challenger against Target. Dummy variable: scored 1 for status quo behavior as most conflictual event, 0 otherwise. Source: WEIS
TradeShare$_{ct}$	Bilateral trade between Challenger and Target divided by Challenger's Total Trade. Continuous variable: 0 indicates no trade, 1 indicates all of Challenger's trade is with Target. Source: IMF Direction of Trade, Barbieri
TradeGDP$_{ct}$	Bilateral trade between Challenger and Target divided by Challenger's GDP. Continuous variable: 0 indicates no trade. Source: IMF DoT and Penn WT, Oneal & Russett
Inelasticity$_{ct}$	Challenger's price inelasticity. Continuous variable: 0 indicates most elastic score, positive values indicate inelasticity. Source: Marquez Bilateral Trade Elasticities
Exit Costs (TotTrade)$_{ct}$	Interaction of TradeShare$_{ct}$ and Inelasticity$_{ct}$.
Exit Costs (GDP)$_{ct}$	Interaction of TradeGDP$_{ct}$ and Inelasticity$_{ct}$.
Capability Ratio$_{ct}$	Ratio of CINC scores with Challenger's score in numerator. Continuous variable, > 0, with 1 indicating total parity. Source: COW, EUGene

Low-level Conflict and Target's Exit Costs

The first model to be estimated evaluates hypothesis 1a: the claim that an increase in the Target's exit costs leads to an increase in low-level conflict initiated by the Challenger. Support for this hypothesis would come in the form of a positive and statistically significant parameter estimate for the *Exit Costs$_{tc}$* variable in equation 5.5. Because studies have shown that import price inelasticity and trade variables can have an independent effect on conflict (Polachek and McDonald, 1992; Barbieri, 1996; Oneal and Russett, 1997; Polachek, 1997; Polachek et al., 1999), I include these independent variables throughout the analysis to ensure the proper estimation of the interactive Exit Costs variables. Equation 5.5 represents the first logit model in the standard logit model structure:

$$\text{Prob (Low Conflict}_{ct} = 1) = \frac{e^{\mu}}{1 + e^{\mu}},$$

$$\mu = \beta_0 + \beta_1 \text{Trade}_{tc} + \beta_2 \text{Inelasticity}_{tc} + \beta_3 \text{Exit Costs}_{tc}$$

(5.5)

For the remaining logit models, I present only the variables and parameters involved, and ask the reader to assume the logit model structure is present.

Table 5.5 displays the estimation results of this first model. Columns 1 and 2 represent the estimation of equation 5.5 using the *TradeShare$_{tc}$* and *TradeGDP$_{tc}$* variables.[9] In both specifications of the model, the parameter estimate for the *ExitCosts$_{tc}$* variable is positive and statistically significant at the $p<0.05$ level, providing support for the prediction that an increase in the Target's exit costs indeed increases the likelihood of low-level conflict. Both model estimations also perform well as a whole, with the Likelihood Ratio tests indicating that the models improve on the null model in their ability to predict the dependent variable.[10]

Equation 5.6 adds the *CapabilityRatio$_{ct}$* variable to the first model, and estimates for this equation are listed in columns 3 and 4 of table 5:

$$\text{Low Conflict}_{ct} = \beta_0 + \beta_1 \text{Trade}_{tc} + \beta_2 \text{Inelasticity}_{tc}$$
$$+ \beta_3 \text{ExitCosts}_{tc} + \beta_4 \text{CapRatio}_{ct}$$

(5.6)

The prediction in hypothesis 3b is that this added variable will be positive. Again, the parameter estimates for the *Exit Costs$_{tc}$* variable are positive and statistically significant at the $p<0.05$ level, indicating support for hypothesis 1a. The parameter estimates for *CapabilityRatio$_{ct}$*, however, are negative and not statistically significant, indicating a lack of support for the hypothesis. Further, the models with the added variable do not significantly increase our ability to predict the dependent variable.

Table 5.5. Logit Estimates of Low-level Conflict

Variable		Eqn (5)	Eqn (5)	Eqn (6)	Eqn (6)
Target's TradeShare	β	**-118.166**		**-105.928**	
	SE$_\beta$	57.793		56.012	
	p	0.021		0.030	
Target's Trade/GDP			**-298.646**		-247.499*
			159.161		168.308
			0.031		0.071
Target's Inelasticity		**-1.683**	**-1.433**	**-1.520**	-1.284
		0.901	0.808	0.900	0.817
		0.031	0.038	0.046	0.058
Target's Exit Costs		**54.834**	**143.121**	**49.998**	**123.609**
		25.411	67.503	24.622	70.460
		0.016	0.017	0.021	0.040
Capability Ratio				-0.337	-0.288
				0.426	0.401
				0.429	0.472
Constant		1.949	1.157	1.970	1.089
		1.741	1.495	1.740	1.498
		0.263	0.439	0.258	0.467
Log Likelihood		-17.592	-17.547	-17.125	-17.192
L R χ^2 (df)		7.47[a] (3)	7.56[a] (3)	0.93[b] (1)	0.71[b] (1)
LR p-value		0.058	0.056	0.334	0.399
Pseudo R2		0.175	0.177	0.197	0.194
N		40	40	40	40

* $p < 0.10$, bold = $p < 0.05$, p-values are one-tailed, except CapRatio and Constant
[a] LR test versus null model, [b] LR test versus model w/o CapRatio

High-level Conflict and Target's Exit Costs

The next logit model examines the claim in hypothesis 2a that an increase in the Target's exit costs leads to a decrease in the likelihood of high-level conflict. Equation 5.7 presents the model specification:

$$\text{High Conflict}_{ct} = \beta_0 + \beta_1 \text{Trade}_{tc} + \beta_2 \text{Inelasticity}_{tc} + \beta_3 \text{Exit Costs}_{tc}. \quad (5.7)$$

The first two columns in table 5.6 represent the model estimation using the *TradeShare* and *TradeGDP* variables. In both models the parameter estimate for the *ExitCosts* variable is negative and statistically significant at the $p<0.05$ level, providing support for the hypothesis. Model diagnostics indicate that both models significantly improve on our ability to predict high-level conflict.

Adding the *CapabilityRatio* control variable to this model changes the model specification to equation 5.8:

$$\text{High Conflict}_{ct} = \beta_0 + \beta_1 \text{Trade}_{tc} + \beta_2 \text{Inelasticity}_{tc} \\ + \beta_3 \text{Exit Costs}_{tc} + \beta_4 \text{CapRatio}_{ct} \quad (5.8)$$

The estimates for this model are in the third and fourth columns of table 5.6. The impact of *ExitCosts* on *High-level Conflict* remains negative and statistically significant, although the significance level of the *TradeGDP* model drops to the $p<0.10$ level. As with the earlier models, the parameter estimates for the *CapabilityRatio* variable are not statistically significant, indicating a lack of support for hypothesis 3a. Similarly, the model diagnostics suggest that the inclusion of the *CapabilityRatio* variable does not significantly improve our ability to predict high-level conflict.

Table 5.6. Logit Estimates of High-level Conflict

Variable		Eqn (7)	Eqn (7)	Eqn (8)	Eqn (8)
Target's TradeShare	β	**139.212**		**126.392**	
	SE$_\beta$	62.604		62.808	
	p	0.013		0.022	
Target's Trade/GDP			**263.799**		241.1397*
			137.398		147.461
			0.028		0.051
Target's Inelasticity		1.9777*	1.046	1.7999*	0.964
		1.326	0.978	1.322	0.989
		0.068	0.143	0.087	0.165
Target's Exit Costs		**-54.524**	**-100.752**	**-49.465**	-91.9606*
		26.385	59.142	26.464	62.660
		0.020	0.044	0.031	0.071
Capability Ratio				0.126	0.079
				0.203	0.196
				0.534	0.686
Constant		-5.5525*	-3.215	-5.3106*	-3.117
		2.865	1.975	2.804	1.968
		0.053	0.104	0.058	0.113
Log Likelihood		-20.669	-23.374	-20.464	-23.291
L R χ^2 (df)		13.71[a] (3)	8.30[a] (3)	0.41[b] (1)	0.17[b] (1)
LR p-value		0.003	0.040	0.522	0.683
Pseudo R2		0.249	0.151	0.257	0.154
N		40	40	40	40

* $p < 0.10$, bold = $p < 0.05$, p-values are one-tailed, except CapRatio and Constant
[a] LR test versus null model, [b] LR test versus model w/o CapRatio

High-level Conflict with Exit Costs for Both States

The first two sections in this analysis were concerned only with the Target state's exit costs as a predictor of low- and high-level conflict. The exit model, however, makes the rather interesting prediction that when it comes to low-level conflict initiated by the Challenger, the exit costs for the Challenger are not a significant factor (H1b). For high-level conflict, on the other hand, the exit model predicts that higher exit costs for the Challenger will have the same negative effect as the Target's exit costs (H2b). I examine this claim regarding high-level conflict here, and the next section returns to low-level conflict.

Including the economic independent variables for the Challenger changes equation 5.7 to the following equation:

$$\text{High Conflict}_{ct} = \beta_0 + \beta_1\text{Trade}_{tc} + \beta_2\text{Inelasticity}_{tc}$$
$$+ \beta_3\text{Exit Costs}_{tc} + \beta_4\text{Trade}_{ct} \qquad (5.9)$$
$$+ \beta_5\text{Inelasticity}_{ct} + \beta_6\text{Exit Costs}_{ct}$$

For this model, I not only expect the Target's exit costs (*ExitCosts_{tc}*) to be negative, the Challenger's exit costs (*ExitCosts_{ct}*) should be negative as well. Estimates of this model using the *TradeShare* and *TradeGDP* variables are included in columns 1 and 2 of table 5.7. The parameter estimates for both variables are in the expected direction, but only the Target's exit costs are statistically significant. Additionally, the likelihood ratio tests indicate that the inclusion of the Challenger variables does not enhance the ability of the model to predict the occurrence of high-level conflict (p=0.259). Thus, while the sign on the parameter estimates for the Challenger's exit costs were in the expected direction, these results do not appear to be robust.

Adding the *CapabilityRatio* control variable to the model leads to similar results. Equation 5.10 contains this model specification with the included economic variables for the Challenger:

$$\text{High Conflict}_{ct} = \beta_0 + \beta_1\text{Trade}_{tc} + \beta_2\text{Inelasticity}_{tc}$$
$$+ \beta_3\text{Exit Costs}_{tc} + \beta_4\text{Trade}_{ct} + \beta_5\text{Inelasticity}_{ct} \qquad (5.10)$$
$$+ \beta_6\text{Exit Costs}_{ct} + \beta_6\text{CapRatio}_{ct}$$

Columns 3 and 4 in table 5.7 display the results of this model. None of the exit costs variables are statistically significant, although they do maintain the expected negative direction in the coefficients. In addition, the estimates for the *CapabilityRatio* variable are positive rather than the predicted negative direction.

Table 5.7. High-level Conflict with Exit Costs for Challenger and Target

Variable		Eqn (9)	Eqn (9)	Eqn (10)	Eqn (10)
Target's TradeShare	β	**132.738**		56.358	
	SE_β	70.317		79.233	
	p	0.030		0.239	
Target's Trade/GDP			**331.619**		113.334
			155.005		151.435
			0.016		0.227
Target's Inelasticity		1.666	1.250	0.621	0.399
		1.409	1.190	1.363	1.237
		0.119	0.147	0.324	0.374
Target's Exit Costs		**-53.808**	**-135.915**	-25.969	-74.530
		28.965	68.511	31.111	65.974
		0.032	0.024	0.202	0.130
Challenger's TradeShare		89.9469*		105.4503*	
		63.319		67.460	
		0.078		0.059	
Challenger's Trade/GDP			218.3527*		**286.156**
			140.983		157.634
			0.061		0.035
Challenger's Inelasticity		0.444	0.239	0.752	0.405
		1.040	0.890	1.130	0.963
		0.335	0.394	0.253	0.674
Challenger's Exit Costs		-30.879	-74.779	-32.686	-65.702
		26.150	61.978	27.376	64.505
		0.119	0.114	0.117	0.154
Capability Ratio				0.455	0.98251*
				0.310	0.510
				0.143	0.054
Constant		-6.8636*	-5.1075*	-5.9334*	-5.5028*
		3.815	3.083	3.576	3.176
		0.072	0.098	0.097	0.083
Log Likelihood		-18.657	-20.331	-17.268	-16.954
L R χ^2 (df)		17.74[a] (6)	14.39[a] (6)	2.78[b] (1)	6.75[b] (1)
Pseudo R^2		0.322	0.261	0.373	0.384
N		40	40	40	40

* $p < 0.10$, bold = $p < 0.05$, 1-tailed p-values

[a] LR test versus null model, [b] LR test versus model w/o CapRatio

Using the *TradeGDP* model this variable is statistically significant at the p<0.10 level.. Unfortunately, this significance adds to the already poor support for the hypothesis (H3b) that the likelihood of success for the Challenger in high-level conflict has a negative impact on the occurrence of this type of conflict.

Low-level Conflict with Exit Costs for Both States

The final set of models examines the prediction of the exit model that the Challenger's exit cost levels do not affect low-level conflict. The inclusion of economic independent variables for the Challenger transforms equation 5.5 into the following:

$$\text{Low Conflict}_{ct} = \beta_0 + \beta_1 \text{Trade}_{tc} + \beta_2 \text{Inelasticity}_{tc} + \beta_3 \text{Exit Costs}_{tc} \\ + \beta_4 \text{Trade}_{ct} + \beta_5 \text{Inelasticity}_{ct} + \beta_6 \text{Exit Costs}_{ct} \quad . \; (5.11)$$

In this model, the expectation is that the added *ExitCost$_{ct}$* variable will not be statistically significant. Table 5.8 displays the estimates of this model using the two trade variable specifications. The results are consistent with the hypothesis (H1b) that the Challenger's exit costs do not have an impact on the incidence of low-level conflict initiated by the Challenger. The addition of the economic variables for the Challenger does not reduce the impact of the Target's exit costs (*ExitCost$_{tc}$*) on low-level conflict, as the model still supports hypothesis 1a.

Finally, adding the *CapabilityRatio* control variable:

$$\text{Low Conflict}_{ct} = \beta_0 + \beta_1 \text{Trade}_{tc} + \beta_2 \text{Inelasticity}_{tc} + \beta_3 \text{Exit Costs}_{tc} \\ + \beta_4 \text{Trade}_{ct} + \beta_5 \text{Inelasticity}_{ct} + \beta_6 \text{Exit Costs}_{ct} \quad (5.12) \\ + \beta_6 \text{CapRatio}_{ct}$$

does not provide any added value to the model in terms of predicting low-level conflict. As with the other analyses that include this variable, the parameter estimate for *CapabilityRatio* is neither statistically significant nor in the expected direction.

The inclusion of the interaction terms (*ExitCost$_{ct}$*, *ExitCost$_{tc}$*) can make the coefficients in these tables difficult to interpret. Figures 5.3 and 5.4 demonstrate graphically how the interaction of trade and inelasticity is critical to the likelihood of low- and high-level conflict. Both figures are generated by varying inelasticity from least to most inelastic, and tradeshare is held at three constant levels (its mean and ± approximately one standard deviation). The effects of the interaction of trade and inelasticity on the likelihood of low-level conflict are represented in figure 5.2, while figure 5.3 displays these effects with respect to high-level conflict. Figure 5.2 shows that when trade is low, an increase in inelasticity reduces the likelihood of low-level conflict. When trade is at its mean, however, the likelihood of low-level conflict remains very low *except* when inelasticity is high. When trade is high, this interactive effect is even more dramatic. Similar results hold in figure 5.3. An increase in inelasticity generates a decrease in the likelihood of high-level conflict only when trade is also at its mean or higher. It is the interaction of trade and inelasticity that generates exit costs, and these exit costs have important effects on the incidence of international conflict.

Table 5.8. Low-level Conflict with Exit Costs for Challenger and Target

Variable		Eqn (11)	Eqn (11)	Eqn (12)	Eqn (12)
Target's TradeShare	β	**-211.962**		-205.7283*	
	SE_β	116.836		144.698	
	p	0.035		0.078	
Target's Trade/GDP			**-526.004**		-440.7375*
			235.760		323.575
			0.013		0.087
Target's Inelasticity		**-2.688**	**-2.154**	-2.6141*	-1.9328*
		1.440	1.116	1.748	1.240
		0.031	0.027	0.068	0.060
Target's Exit Costs		**90.530**	**239.799**	88.19*	**214.629**
		47.233	104.718	57.026	123.166
		0.028	0.011	0.061	0.041
Challenger's TradeShare		-23.538		-24.905	
		147.795		148.556	
		0.437		0.434	
Challenger's Trade/GDP			-262.336		-275.773
			387.352		403.313
			0.249		0.247
Challenger's Inelasticity		6.1027*	4.541	5.9907*	4.364
		4.139	3.692	4.403	3.818
		0.070	0.110	0.087	0.253
Challenger's Exit Costs		6.881	91.524	7.206	86.099
		60.072	155.448	60.056	162.278
		0.455	0.278	0.452	0.298
Capability Ratio				-0.054	-0.352
				0.747	0.982
				0.942	0.720
Constant		-8.475	-6.289	-8.313	-5.887
		8.435	7.910	8.722	8.203
		0.315	0.427	0.341	0.473
Log Likelihood		-11.949	-11.640	-11.946	-11.568
L R χ^2 (df)		**18.75**[a] (6)	**19.37**[a] (6)	0.01[b] (1)	0.14[b] (1)
Pseudo R^2		0.440	0.454	0.440	0.458
N		40	40	40	40

* p<0.10, bold = p<0.05, 1-tailed p-values except CapRatio and Constant

[a] LR test versus null model, [b] LR test versus model w/o CapRatio

Figure 5.2. Effect of Inelasticity on Low-level Conflict when Trade is Low/Mean/High

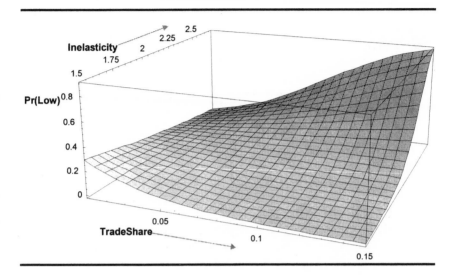

Figure 5.3. Effect of Inelasticity on High-level Conflict when Trade is Low/Mean/High

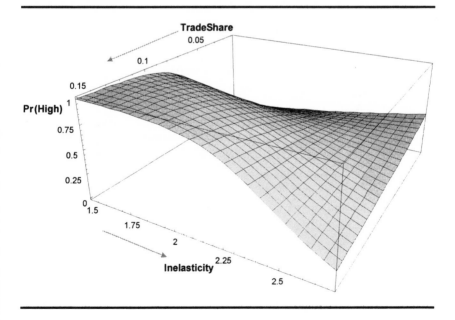

Conclusion

Recent research on the interdependence-conflict puzzle has largely relied on large-n quantitative methods to search for answers (Barbieri, 1996; Oneal and Russett, 1997). The concept of economic exit as the defining characteristic of interdependence suggests that the measurements employed by Barbieri and Oneal and Russett are closer to measurements of trade intensity than interdependence. The logical structure of their regression models misses the complex relationship between interdependence and conflict that is predicted by the exit model. At the cost of sample size, time series analysis, and breadth in spatial domain, this study has instead focused on a more valid operationalization (although still imperfect) of economic interdependence and a more complex relationship between this interdependence and political conflict.

Support for the hypotheses derived above indicates that the predictions that emerge from the exit model provide new and interesting information about the interdependence-conflict relationship in the real world. Although this analysis supports the exit model, more research is needed. The limited spatial scope of the inelasticity data selected out any dyads that have experienced war in the last three decades. Expanding the set of available dyads for analysis to include dyads that are not both democratic, have fought wars, and are less economically active would strengthen the ability of the statistical analyses to make more general claims about the causal relationship between interdependence and conflict. Another profitable direction for future empirical research would be to examine one pair of states over time to see how changes in the economic interdependence between the two states affects their conflictual behavior toward one another. This design would allow the researcher to focus more specifically on the changes in political behavior that are affected by the economic relationship, as issues of cross-sectional research design are not relevant.

Future research, whether it is time-series or expanded cross-sectional in nature, will be able to take advantage of the theoretical platform established by the exit model. This model informs the way we think about economic interdependence and political conflict, and it will serve as a useful tool for the study of international relations.

Notes

1. Of course, the independence of the cost of conflict from the probability of success can be a difficult assumption to maintain. Costs are likely to vary with respect to who wins and who loses a military conflict. I choose to reflect the difference in these costs in the exit model with the understanding that states will investigate the costs and likelihood of success concurrently. Thus, adding additional cost variables for success and failure would be redundant from an analytical perspective, despite the added accuracy in terms of the logic of the model.
2. Washington apples are considered a delicacy in Japan.
3. Polachek (1997) and Polachek, Chang, and Robst (1999) set a precedent for the extraction of Italy and France from the "ROECD" group. Since, however, both states will have identical elasticity vectors, I do not include the France-Italy or Italy-France dyads in this study.
4. Maximum trade values were also used with similar results.
5. Goldstein (1992) adapts these sixty-one categories into a conflict-cooperation scale. His scale ranges from -10 as the most conflictual event to 8.3 as the most cooperative. The categories employed in this study can easily be mapped to the Goldstein WEIS scale: events ranging from +8.3 to -3.4 are coded as status quo events; events ranging from -3.4 to -6.9 are low-level conflict events; and the events ranging from -7.0 to -10.0 are high-level conflict events. In this sense, the three categories employed here can also be considered a rough scale.
6. This is the basic coding rule for the MIDs data, to report the highest level of hostility in any given dyad-year. An alternative method of using the average level of conflict with respect to the three categories of status quo and low- and high-level conflict produced similar results.
7. Missing data is not treated as zero capability. It is eliminated from the averaging step.
8. I use the likelihood-ratio test specified in King (1989: 84-5), $\Re = 2(\ln L^* - \ln LR^*)$, where $\Re$ is the likelihood ratio test statistic, $\ln L^*$ is the log-likelihood of the unrestricted model, and $\ln LR^*$ is the log-likelihood of the restricted model. A $\chi 2$ test is used to examine whether the restricted and unrestricted log-likelihood functions are statistically different.
9. The large differences in parameter size are due to variances in the range of values for the three economic independent variables. TradeShare ranges from 0.008 to 0.632, Trade/GDP ranges from 0.002 to 0.273, and Inelasticity ranges from 0 to 2.73. The parameter size compensates for these differences in magnitude, but one needs to compare the relative size of parameter estimates in conjunction with the relative magnitude of the raw data. See the Summary Statistics table in the Appendix.

10. Nesting a model with only the independent trade and inelasticity variables within a model with these variables and the exit cost variable indicates that the inclusion of the exit cost variable significantly improves the prediction of the dependent variable ($p=0.006$). This result also holds for high-level conflict as the dependent variable ($p=0.014$).

6
Conclusion:
Implications of the Exit Model in a Globalized World

The initial challenge set forth in this book was to answer the question of whether economic interdependence leads to an increase or decrease in political conflict, or if it has no effect. The question is far from new. It can even be considered the common motivating question driving current research in this area. Despite this focus, there remains a persistent debate in the literature regarding which of the three possible answers is correct. At the end of this book, my answer to this question is, of course, all three.

This answer would be useless to the social scientist if not for the fact that the theoretical progress made here provides us with the tools necessary to specify *when* each type of relationship between interdependence and conflict is expected. Thus, while the puzzle of the economic interdependence-political conflict relationship is not new, the solutions developed here are. The result is that the study of economic interdependence and political conflict can now move beyond correlation studies and build from the theoretical platform provided by the exit model in chapter 3. In these remaining pages I would like to revisit the contributions of this book, its limitations, and avenues for future research.

Understanding Economic Interdependence

The term *economic interdependence* has been used to represent a broad and often vague range of economic interstate behavior. Occasionally the term becomes out of fashion, and it is currently competing with such terms as *globalization* and *internationalization*. The willingness in the literature to interchange terminology has hindered our ability to study the relationship between economics and politics. By returning to the classic definition of interdependence as a function of exit costs, a definition first set forth by Hirschman (1945) and echoed by Keohane and Nye (1989) and Baldwin (1980), I was better equipped to develop the exit model. In order to focus our understanding of both the concept of economic interdependence and the relationship between economic interdependence and political conflict, I pushed this concept further than its classic definition. The goal was to provide enough detail about economic interdependence to be able to identify situations of interdependence using abstract rules. In this respect, I have fleshed out a very intuitive but surprisingly elusive concept.

An important consequence of this focus is that this book became a study of one particular dimension of economic exchange and its influence on political conflict. By defining economic interdependence narrowly—as a function of exit costs driven by market structure and asset specificity—I developed a more solid conceptual foundation that was helpful during the theoretical development of the exit model. At the same time, we should recognize that other dimensions of economic exchange might also influence political conflict. For example, the phenomena of economic exchange may produce non-strategic effects that condition states toward or away from political conflict. International trade may lead to cultural understanding that fosters peace, or it may lead to the discovery of new and enticing foreign resources that lead to imperialism. The point is that economic ties between nations are complex, and the progress made here leads to a partial understanding of the overall relationship between the economic and political dimensions of world politics.

The Economic Interdependence-Political Conflict Relationship

With the humble understanding that this book investigates a piece of a larger puzzle, let us assess the progress made toward a working theory of economic interdependence and political conflict. The focus on exit costs and the exit option leads to a natural question about when states may be able to use this exit option for political gain and how they go about exercising this leverage. The exit model developed in chapter 3 is a theory of how potential exit costs can become tools of political manipulation for states to use in extracting demands from one another. By placing exit costs within the broader cost-benefit analysis of the political alternatives states face in political situations, the model demonstrates that interdependence can lead to bargaining power. It also demonstrates that economic interdependence can constrain a state from making political demands, but sometimes the economic ties between two states are insufficient to constrain states from turning to the military arena to settle their disputes.

The analysis of the model reveals an interesting interaction between potential exit costs and the willingness of states to endure these costs in the event of a dispute. Both the Challenger and the Target have exit cost thresholds that limit the exit costs they are willing to bear. These thresholds are a function of the value each state associates with the issue at stake in the Challenger's demands, the costs of escalating to high levels of conflict to resolve the dispute, and the likelihood that the outcome of such escalation will be favorable to one state or the other. The relationship between potential exit costs and the exit cost threshold, combined with the same relationship for the other state, are what determine each state's strategy in the game.

It is this interaction—between the exit costs and the exit cost thresholds-that provides a fundamental contribution to the literature. Only by considering the exit costs of each state relative to the costs it is willing to endure do we begin to tease out a more complex understanding of *when* economic interdependence constrains states from entering into high levels of political conflict. There are two significant advances here. First, we are now able to move away from the basic agenda of identifying the presence and direction of a relationship between economic interdependence and political conflict. The analysis of the exit model shifts our attention to the more nuanced puzzle of ascertaining when the political-economic conditions are ripe for a state to successfully employ the threat of economic exit to extract demands without the risk of militarized political conflict. Second, the process of translating the economic interdependence-political conflict relationship into a formal model provides us with much-needed clarity in viewing the causal linkage between the two phenomena. This clarity is a contribution on its own, but it also provides new and focused tools for research. For example, the exit model not only highlights the importance of locating exit costs relative to the exit cost thresholds; it provides the functional forms for these thresholds. These functions lead to new avenues for empirical research, as demonstrated in chapters 4 and 5.

Empirical Support for the Exit Model

The qualitative and quantitative methods complement one another in the empirical analysis. The case histories in chapter 4 allow the reader to get a firm grip on the strategic interaction in the exit model and they provide a superior lens to view a state's perception of its own exit cost thresholds. This internal validity, however, comes at a price. The case histories provide an excellent assessment of how the exit model can inform our understanding of real world events, but case selection eliminates our confidence in the analysis as a test of the model.

The statistical analysis in chapter 5, on the other hand, provides a test of the implications of the exit model. Although the model is not tested as an entire theory, the fundamental predictions emerging from the formal analysis of the model are tested separately. This approach sacrifices the internal validity found in chapter 4 for the ability to come to more systematic and rigorous conclusions about the performance of the exit model in the real world. Despite this two-pronged empirical assessment, the exercise of evaluating the exit model reveals some of the limitations of the exit model as well as several avenues for future research.

Future Research

More research is needed to improve upon the exit model as an abstract representation of real-world strategic interaction. At the same time, expanded data analysis and diverse empirical methodologies need to continue to be applied to the theoretical arguments developed here and in the future. In this section, I briefly outline some possible directions for future theoretical and empirical research.

Generalizing the Exit Model

The exit model presented in chapter 3 tells a basic story of dyadic interstate interaction that is informed by market structure and intrastate adaptation. Several of the assumptions that went into building this model, however, limit the applicability of the model to the empirical world. One such limitation results from the assumption that both states are aware of each other's exit cost and exit cost thresholds. With this information, they are able to predict exactly what the other state would do for any given strategy of their own. No bluffing takes place, and no opportunities are missed. Indeed, one conclusion we can draw from this assumption is that when states have full information regarding economic interdependence, economic exit never occurs unless it is a step on the path to higher levels of conflict.

The real world is full of situations where economic exit occurred without higher levels of conflict. One important example is the grain embargo instituted by the United States against the Soviet Union in January of 1980. In this situation, President Carter threatened a grain embargo unless the Soviets withdrew from their invasion of Afghanistan. The Soviets refused, and the United States imposed the embargo. Of the seventeen million tons of grain denied to the Soviets by the United States, the Soviets were able to find substitute markets to purchase all but six million tons of the original seventeen. Countries such as Argentina, Australia, Canada, and the European Community supplied the substitute grain, and the U.S. embargo was considered a failure (Becker, 1984). Most importantly, the United States did not choose to escalate the issue through the use or threat of military force. Instead, President Reagan lifted the embargo in April of 1981.

There are three explanations of the discord between this case and the equilibrium behavior specified in the exit model in chapter 3. First, one could conclude that President Carter moved off the equilibrium path and behaved irrationally. Second, it is possible that the audience costs faced by the United States in this situation were different than what is generally discussed in the exit model. Specifically, the United States may have faced audience costs for *not* imposing the embargo which were greater than the audience costs it incurred from imposing the embargo and then backing down. Finally, a third explanation is that President Carter and the United States gambled when they picked their strategy, and they had incomplete knowledge regarding the Soviets' ability to recoup the losses imposed by the embargo. The second and third explanations make good candidates for future research.

Whether internationally or domestically incurred, audience costs are an important piece of the decision calculus for political leaders. Internationally, leaders seek to preserve their credibility and reputation. Domestically, leaders seek to maintain successful foreign policy portfolios to ensure their political survival. During the Cold War, the United States and the Soviet Union often went to great lengths to demonstrate to the world that each side was resolved to oppose the other along any public dimension. Backing down is never seen as an ideal outcome for anyone, but sometimes doing nothing and remaining at the status quo is frowned upon even more. The exit model can be adapted to capture this complex wrinkle by adjusting the relationship between one or both states' utilities associated with the status quo and backing down. Currently, backing down provides a strictly negative utility, while the status quo is normalized to zero. In short, the status quo is always preferred to backing down. One alternative would be to adjust the utilities of the Challenger (the United States in the example of Carter's grain embargo) such that backing down is preferred to remaining at the status quo. An additional move can also be afforded to the Challenger where it has the option to back down after exiting the economic relationship if the Target continues to reject the Challenger's demands. This configuration may lead to situations where the Challenger has an incentive to exit the economic relationship to minimize audience costs, but the Challenger has no intention of escalating the dispute to militarized levels.

A second avenue for expanding the exit model is to introduce private information for one or both players in the game. This private information concerns the value each state places on the issue at stake in the Challenger's demand. A higher utility for either state leads to a higher exit cost threshold, thereby making it more likely that the economic relationship fails to constrain the Challenger from making the demand or forcing the Target to yield to the Challenger's threat of exit. If the utility each state associates with the demand is private information, held only by the state itself and not known by the opponent, then each state has an incentive to mislead the other. The Challenger has an incentive to issue a demand and threat of exit even though it knows the exit costs exceed its threshold. Similarly, the Target has an incentive to bluff and reject the Challenger's demand even though the Target knows it cannot endure the costs of exit. If either player çan improve its situation through false pretenses, it will seek to do so. As such, the story takes on an added dimension of signaling and cheap talk.

Expanding the Empirical Investigation

Along with these theoretical avenues, there are also several tasks remaining in the realm of empirical research. Beyond the general utility in expanded case histories, two principal directions may prove to be fruitful. First, the set of available cases for large-n analysis needs breadth and diversity. The set of cases delimited by Marquez's inelasticity data provides an adequate first cut at testing the hypotheses in chapter 5, but several limitations need to be overcome. Cases involving dyads that are not democratic and not major trading partners would help to generalize the results beyond the advanced industrialized countries. Cases involving dyads that have fought wars and engaged in militarized disputes would enable the statistical analyses to see if the relationships predicted by the exit model also hold in situations where extreme conflict resulted. Expanding the inelasticity data will be difficult, but the payoff is greater confidence in the generalizability of the results.

The second path for empirical research involves generating data for pairs of states across time where all the variables are indeed variables. Currently, the inelasticity data is in cross-sectional form, while the trade data is aggregated to yearly units and political conflict data ranges from daily (at least, hypothetically) to yearly aggregations. Information on import price inelasticities that varies at least on a yearly basis would allow the researcher to study how changes in economic interdependence across time within a dyad lead to changes in political behavior. This approach would maximize the researcher's ability to focus on changes in economic interdependence while holding other factors constant.

Tools of Adaptation: Conflict, Cooperation, and Integration

Beyond these direct expansions of the work presented here, another dimension of the economic interdependence-political conflict puzzle remains unexplored. Given the exit model and the behavior it predicts from states, under what circumstances does economic interdependence motivate a state to change the economic situation? Will this motivation lead to cooperation or the establishment of international regimes such as the World Trade Organization (WTO), designed to promote healthy market structure that minimizes the costly effects of interdependence? Or will this motivation lead to the decision to try to use force to remove the vulnerabilities that interdependence can bring, as Iraq did in its invasion of Kuwait in 1990? The anticipation of what the game will bring in terms of political behavior can motivate states to act before the exit model is played. Whether this action is cooperative or conflictual is an exciting question that remains to be explored.

Implications for a Globalized World

If the lessons of the exit model inform us about the direct dyadic relationship among nations and their propensities to use force, what does it say about the occurrence of conflict in the global system of nations? More specifically, if we can define the term "globalization" to mean an increase in economic and informational exchange across national borders, how then does an increase in globalization influence the level of violence in the system?

This is a complicated question with many facets to hold constant. But since concluding chapters are designed for musing, let us assume we can hold the many factors of globalization (and the institutions that govern these factors) constant and focus on how interdependence may play a role. Through this lens it is possible to make some predictions about the aggregate impact of economic interdependence.

The key to this impact is an assumption about what globalization will do to the market structure within which states interact economically. Recall that the costs of economic exit are high when two nations engage in economic exchange that involves high levels of asset specificity that make it harder for one or both states to find alternatives to their current situation. The question then becomes this: does globalization make markets more or less adaptable, and does globalization make economic exchange more or less asset specific?

There is reason to believe that globalization will make economic exchange more asset specific and markets less adaptable. This is a counterintuitive position to take, as globalization typically makes us think of increased competition and increased choice. But consider two points, both based on the assumption that efficiency will be a motivating factor in globalization. First, economic units (firms) are under constant pressure (through competition) to become more efficient, and this efficiency can lead to specialization. Specialization, especially if it occurs across borders, can lead to a decrease in market flexibility and an increase in asset specificity. While this asset specificity should be less permanent than situations of specificity that are driven by allocations of natural resources, the costs of adaptation may still be large enough to influence policy.

Second, as free markets develop across the global system, the natural drive toward monopolistic competition will be more difficult to check. One of the central roles of the state has historically been to prevent the formation of domestic monopolies. If we assume that international governmental organizations will take on the charge of preventing monopolies in international economic relationships, then there is cause for concern. That is because international organizations are rarely (if ever) as powerful as domestic governments.

If this path is taken, then market structure will become less flexible as a result of globalization, not more so. The costs of adaptation will increase as a result, making real cases of economic interdependence more prevalent in the system. Such an increase in economic interdependence will not lead to improved harmony among nations, but it will generate more opportunities to use the economic relationship as an alternative arena for contestation. The implication from the exit model is that militarized conflict should decrease as a result.

Final Words

In the end, this book breaks new ground in the study of economic interdependence and political conflict. We can now move beyond the pursuit of a basic relationship between these two phenomena and build upon the exit model. This progress was accomplished by tackling the questions of what economic interdependence really entails in an interstate relationship and how it might be linked to political conflict. The answers to these questions come together to provide an answer to why economic interdependence sometimes has a pacific effect on political interaction, sometimes has a conflictual effect, and sometimes has no effect at all.

No umbrella theory of realism or liberalism (or any variant thereof) is required to answer this question. More importantly, the exit model not only reveals the complexity of the relationship between economic interdependence and political conflict; it also provides the researcher with the necessary information to determine *when* a particular equilibrium solution should be expected in the real world. It represents a small step towards a deeper, more focused understanding of the relationship between international economic exchange and political conflict, and its richness is reflected in the many more puzzles that have begun to present themselves.

Appendix

Table A.1. Summary Statistics

Variable	Obs	Mean	Std. Dev	Min	Max
Trade/Total Trade	40	0.08	0.11	0.009	0.63
Trade/GDP	40	0.03	0.04	0.002	0.27
Inelasticity	40	1.92	0.63	0	2.73
Exit Costs (TotTrade)	40	0.16	0.21	0	1.17
Exit Costs (GDP)	40	0.05	0.08	0	0.5
Capability Ratio	40	1.97	2.59	0.08	11.94
Status Quo	40			0	1
Low-level Conflict	40			0	1
High-level Conflict	40			0	1

Table A.2. Correlations

Variables	$\text{Trade}_{tc}/\text{TotTrade}_t$	Inelasticity_t	Exit Costs $(\text{TotTrade})_t$	$\text{Trade}_{ct}/\text{TotTrade}_c$	Inelasticity_c	Exit Costs $(\text{TotTrade})_c$	Capability Ratio
$\text{Trade}_{tc}/\text{TotTrade}_t$	1						
Inelasticity_t	0.1723	1					
Exit Costs $(\text{TotTrade})_t$	0.9859	0.2848	1				
$\text{Trade}_{ct}/\text{TotTrade}_c$	0.4611	0.1599	0.4654	1			
Inelasticity_c	0.1599	0.0414	0.1841	0.1723	1		
Exit Costs $(\text{TotTrade})_c$	0.4654	0.1841	0.4738	0.9859	0.2848	1	
Capability Ratio	0.5907	0.0876	0.5526	-0.0692	-0.1282	-0.0929	1

Variables	$\text{Trade}_{tc}/\text{GDP}_t$	Inelasticity_t	Exit Costs $(\text{GDP})_t$	$\text{Trade}_{ct}/\text{GDP}_c$	Inelasticity_c	Exit Costs $(\text{GDP})_c$	Capability Ratio
$\text{Trade}_{tc}/\text{GDP}_t$	1						
Inelasticity_t	0.157	1					
Exit Costs $(\text{GDP})_t$	0.99	0.2484	1				
$\text{Trade}_{ct}/\text{GDP}_c$	0.0948	0.1578	0.1182	1			
Inelasticity_c	0.1578	0.0414	0.1868	0.157	1		
Exit Costs $(\text{GDP})_c$	0.1182	0.1868	0.1489	0.99	0.2484	1	
Capability Ratio	0.6707	0.0876	0.6398	-0.2178	-0.1282	-0.2382	1

Table A.3. Data (Source: Marquez 1990)

Ddyad	Trade-Share$_{ct}$	Trade-Share$_{tc}$	GDP$_c$	GDP$_t$	Trade$_{ct}$	Trade$_{ct}$/GDP$_t$
uscan	0.190	0.633	83,028,229	7,797,619	2,126,739	0.026
usuk	0.049	0.116	83,028,229	12,575,712	547,508	0.007
usfra	0.033	0.073	83,028,229	15,221,958	372,485	0.004
usger	0.057	0.075	83,028,229	16,758,646	635,284	0.008
usita	0.025	0.074	83,028,229	11,996,324	285,416	0.003
usjpn	0.151	0.271	83,028,229	33,721,645	1,693,750	0.020
canus	0.633	0.190	7,797,619	83,028,229	2,126,739	0.273
canuk	0.035	0.025	7,797,619	12,575,712	117,013	0.015
canfra	0.013	0.009	7,797,619	15,221,958	43,818	0.006
canger	0.022	0.009	7,797,619	16,758,646	74,849	0.010
canita	0.011	0.010	7,797,619	11,996,324	37,321	0.005
canjpn	0.060	0.032	7,797,619	33,721,645	202,375	0.026
ukus	0.116	0.049	12,575,712	83,028,229	547,508	0.044
ukcan	0.025	0.035	12,575,712	7,797,619	117,013	0.009
ukfra	0.081	0.075	12,575,712	15,221,958	381,917	0.030
ukger	0.162	0.070	12,575,712	16,758,646	598,000	0.048
ukita	0.046	0.057	12,575,712	11,996,324	219,932	0.017
ukjpn	0.037	0.028	12,575,712	33,721,645	173,112	0.014
fraus	0.073	0.033	15,221,958	83,028,229	372,485	0.024
fracan	0.009	0.013	15,221,958	7,797,619	43,818	0.003
frauk	0.075	0.081	15,221,958	12,575,712	381,917	0.025
frager	0.151	0.090	15,221,958	16,758,646	769,599	0.051
frajpn	0.025	0.021	15,221,958	33,721,645	128,352	0.008
gerus	0.075	0.057	16,758,646	83,028,229	635,284	0.038
gercan	0.009	0.022	16,758,646	7,797,619	74,849	0.004
geruk	0.070	0.162	16,758,646	12,575,712	598,000	0.036
gerfra	0.090	0.151	16,758,646	15,221,958	769,599	0.046
gerita	0.086	0.190	16,758,646	11,996,324	733,637	0.044
gerjpn	0.032	0.044	16,758,646	33,721,645	272,971	0.016
itaus	0.074	0.025	11,996,324	83,028,229	285,416	0.024
itacan	0.010	0.011	11,996,324	7,797,619	37,321	0.003
itauk	0.057	0.046	11,996,324	12,575,712	219,932	0.018
itager	0.190	0.086	11,996,324	16,758,646	733,637	0.061
itajpn	0.019	0.012	11,996,324	33,721,645	71,763	0.006
jpnus	0.271	0.151	33,721,645	83,028,229	1,693,750	0.050
jpncan	0.032	0.060	33,721,645	7,797,619	202,375	0.006
jpnuk	0.028	0.037	33,721,645	12,575,712	173,112	0.005
jpnfra	0.021	0.025	33,721,645	15,221,958	128,352	0.004
jpnger	0.044	0.032	33,721,645	16,758,646	272,971	0.008
jpnita	0.012	0.019	33,721,645	11,996,324	71,763	0.002

Table A.3. Data (Cont.)

Ddyad	Trade$_{ct}$/GDP$_t$	Inelasticity$_{ct}$	Inelasticity$_{tc}$	ExitCosts$_{ct}$ (TotTrade)	ExitCosts$_{tc}$ (TotTrade)
uscan	0.273	2.04	1.85	.39	1.17
usuk	0.044	2.50	1.96	.12	.23
usfra	0.024	1.67	2.12	.06	.15
usger	0.038	1.14	1.95	.06	.15
usita	0.024	1.67	2.12	.04	.16
usjpn	0.050	1.71	2.12	.26	.58
canus	0.026	1.85	2.04	1.17	.39
canuk	0.009	2.38	1.22	.08	.03
canfra	0.003	1.11	1.93	.01	.02
canger	0.004	2.00	2.17	.04	.02
canita	0.003	1.11	1.93	.01	.02
canjpn	0.006	1.56	2.48	.09	.08
ukus	0.007	1.96	2.50	.23	.12
ukcan	0.015	1.22	2.38	.03	.08
ukfra	0.025	2.71	2.29	.22	.17
ukger	0.036	2.35	2.73	.38	.19
ukita	0.018	2.71	2.29	.13	.13
ukjpn	0.005	2.55	2.10	.09	.06
fraus	0.004	2.12	1.67	.15	.06
fracan	0.006	1.93	1.11	.02	.01
frauk	0.030	2.29	2.71	.17	.22
frager	0.046	2.58	2.11	.39	.19
frajpn	0.004	2.06	.00	.05	.00
gerus	0.008	1.95	1.14	.15	.06
gercan	0.010	2.17	2.00	.02	.04
geruk	0.048	2.73	2.35	.19	.38
gerfra	0.051	2.11	2.58	.19	.39
gerita	0.061	2.11	2.58	.18	.49
gerjpn	0.008	1.33	1.53	.04	.07
itaus	0.003	2.12	1.67	.16	.04
itacan	0.005	1.93	1.11	.02	.01
itauk	0.017	2.29	2.71	.13	.13
itager	0.044	2.58	2.11	.49	.18
itajpn	0.002	2.06	.00	.04	.00
jpnus	0.020	2.12	1.71	.58	.26
jpncan	0.026	2.48	1.56	.08	.09
jpnuk	0.014	2.10	2.55	.06	.09
jpnfra	0.008	.00	2.06	.00	.05
jpnger	0.016	1.53	1.33	.07	.04
jpnita	0.006	.00	2.06	.00	.04

Table A.3. Data (Cont.)

Ddyad	ExitCosts$_{ct}$ (GDP)	ExitCosts$_{tc}$ (GDP)	CapRatio$_{ct}$	SQ	Low Conflict	High Conflict
uscan	.05	.50	11.94	0	0	1
usuk	.02	.09	6.19	0	0	1
usfra	.01	.05	7.74	0	0	1
usger	.01	.07	5.65	0	0	1
usita	.01	.05	8.43	0	0	1
usjpn	.03	.11	3.20	0	0	1
canus	.50	.05	0.08	0	0	1
canuk	.04	.01	0.52	0	1	0
canfra	.01	.01	0.65	0	0	1
canger	.02	.01	0.40	1	0	0
canita	.01	.01	0.71	1	0	0
canjpn	.04	.01	0.27	1	0	0
ukus	.09	.02	0.16	0	0	1
ukcan	.01	.04	1.93	1	0	0
ukfra	.08	.06	1.25	0	1	0
ukger	.11	.10	0.91	0	1	0
ukita	.05	.04	1.36	0	1	0
ukjpn	.04	.01	0.52	1	0	0
fraus	.05	.01	0.13	0	0	1
fracan	.01	.01	1.54	0	1	0
frauk	.06	.08	0.80	0	0	1
frager	.13	.10	0.70	0	0	1
frajpn	.02	.00	0.41	0	1	0
gerus	.07	.01	0.18	0	0	1
gercan	.01	.02	2.50	0	0	1
geruk	.10	.11	1.10	0	1	0
gerfra	.10	.13	1.44	0	0	1
gerita	.09	.16	1.80	0	1	0
gerjpn	.02	.01	0.63	1	0	0
itaus	.05	.01	0.12	0	0	1
itacan	.01	.01	1.42	1	0	0
itauk	.04	.05	0.73	0	1	0
itager	.16	.09	0.56	0	0	1
itajpn	.01	.00	0.38	1	0	0
jpnus	.11	.03	0.31	0	0	1
jpncan	.01	.04	3.73	1	0	0
jpnuk	.01	.04	1.93	1	0	0
jpnfra	.00	.02	2.42	1	0	0
jpnger	.01	.02	1.59	1	0	0
jpnita	.00	.01	2.64	1	0	0

Bibliography

Alston, L. J. 1996. "Empirical Work in Institutional Economics: An Overview." In *Empirical Studies in Institutional Change*, edited by L. J. Alston, T. Eggertsson, and D. C. North, 25-30. Cambridge: Cambridge University Press.

Alston, L. J., T. Eggertsson, and D. C. North, eds. 1996. *Empirical Studies in Institutional Change*. Cambridge: Cambridge University Press.

Angell, S. N. 1914. *The Foundations of International Polity*. London: William Heinemann.

Anti-Apartheid Movement. 1986. *A Tiny Little Bit: An Assessment of Britain's Record of Action Against South Africa*. London: Anti-Apartheid Movement.

Baldwin, D. 1980. "Interdependence and Power: A Conceptual Analysis." *International Organization* 34: 471-506.

————. 1985. *Economic Statecraft*. Princeton, NJ: Princeton University Press.

Barbieri, K. 1995. *Economic Interdependence and Militarized Interstate Conflict, 1870-1985*. Ph.D. Dissertation, Political Science. Binghamton, NY: State University of New York, Binghamton.

————. 1996. "Economic Interdependence: A Path to Peace or a Source of Interstate Conflict?" *Journal of Peace Research* 33: 29-49.

————. 2002. *The Liberal Illusion: Does Trade Promote Peace?* Ann Arbor: University of Michigan Press.

Barbieri, K., and J. Levy. 1999. "Sleeping with the Enemy: The Impact of War on Trade." *Journal of Peace Research* 36: 463-79.

160 *Bibliography*

Barfield, C. 1994. "U.S.-China Trade and Investment in the 1990s." In *Beyond MFN: Trade with China and American Interests*, edited by J. Lilley and W. Willkie II. Washington, DC: AEI Press.

Bates, R. H., A. Greif, M. Levi, J.-L. Rosenthal, and B. R. Weingast, eds. 1998. *Analytic Narratives*. Princeton, NJ: Princeton University Press.

Beck, N., J. Katz, and R. Tucker. 1998. "Taking Time Seriously: Time-Series-Cross-Section Analysis with a Binary Dependent Variable." *American Journal of Political Science* 42: 1260-88.

Becker, A. S. 1984. *Economic Leverage on the Soviet Union in the 1980s*. Santa Monica, CA: Rand Corporation.

Beukes, T. 1987. "The Role of Minerals in South African-United States Relations." In *United States-South African Relations: Past, Present and Future*, edited by P. H. Kapp and G. C. Olivier. Cape Town: South Africa: Tafelerg Publishers.

Brecher, M., and J. Wilkenfeld. 1997. *A Study of Crisis*. Ann Arbor: University of Michigan Press.

Brewer, J., and A. Hunter. 1989. *Multimethod Research: A Synthesis of Styles*. Newbury Park, CA: Sage Publications.

Bureau of Export Administration, U.S. Department of Commerce. 1999. *U.S. Commercial Technology Transfers to the Peoples Republic of China*, Bureau of Export Administration, U.S. Department of Commerce.

Buzan, B. 1984. "Economic Structure and International Security: The Limits of the Liberal Case." *International Organization* 38: 597-624.

Carmines, E. G., and R. A. Zeller. 1979. *Reliability and Validity Assessment*. London: Sage Publications.

Cook, T. D., and D. T. Campbell. 1979. *Quasi-Experimentation*. Chicago: Rand McNally.

Cooper, R. N. 1985. "Economic Interdependence and Coordination of Economic Policies." In *Handbook of International Economics, Vol. II*, edited by R. W. Jones and P. B. Kenen, 1196-1234. Amsterdam: North-Holland Press.

Copeland, D. 1996. "Economic Interdependence and War: A Theory of Trade Expectations." *International Security* 20: 5-41.

Crescenzi, M. 1999. "Violence and Uncertainty in Transitions." *Journal of Conflict Resolution* 43: 192-212.

David, M. 1982. "United States-South African Relations: 1962-67." In *Economic Coercion and U.S. Foreign Policy: Implications of Case Studies from the Johnson Administration*, edited by S. Weintraub. Boulder, CO: Westview.

Dillon, G. M. 1989. *The Falklands, Politics, and War*. London: MacMillan Press.

Domke, W. 1988. *War and the Changing Global System*. New Haven, CT: Yale University Press.

Fearon, J. 1994. "Signaling versus the Balance of Power and Interests." *Journal of Conflict Resolution* 38: 236-69.

Freedman, L., and V. Gamba-Stonehouse. 1990. *Signals of War: The Falklands Conflict of 1982*. London: Faber and Faber.

Gamba, V. 1987. *The Falklands/Malvinas War: A Model for North-South Conflict Prevention*. Boston: Allen & Unwin.

Gartzke, E. 2003. "The Classic Liberals Were Just Lucky: A Few Thoughts about Interdependence and Peace." In *Economic Interdependence and International Conflict: New Perspectives on an Enduring Debate*, edited by E. Mansfield and B. Pollins. Ann Arbor: University of Michigan Press.

Gasiorowski, M. 1986. "Economic Interdependence and International Conflict: Some Cross-National Evidence." *International Studies Quarterly* 30: 23-38.

Gerth, J. 1998. "U.S. Knew China Military Used Civilian Satellites, Reports Show." *The New York Times,* June 13, 1998.

Gibbons, R. 1992. *Game Theory for Applied Economists*. Princeton, NJ: Princeton University Press.

Gill, B., and T. Kim 1995. *China's Arms Acquisitions from Abroad: A Quest for 'Superb and Secret Weapons'*. New York: Oxford University Press.

Gilpin, R. 1987. *The Political Economy of International Relations*. Princeton, NJ: Princeton University Press.

Goldstein, J. 1992. "A Conflict-Cooperation Scale for WEIS Events Data." *Journal of Conflict Resolution* 36: 369-85.

Gowa, J. 1994. *Allies, Adversaries and International Trade*. Princeton, NJ: Princeton University Press.

Grieco, J. 1993. "Anarchy and the Limits of Cooperation: A Realist Critique of the Newest Liberal Institutionalism." In *Neorealism and Neoliberalism: The Contemporary Debate*, edited by D. Baldwin. New York: Columbia University Press.

Harsanyi, J. 1977. *Rational Behavior and Bargaining Equilibrium in Games and Social Situations*. New York: Cambridge University Press.

Hart, J. 1976. "Three Approaches to the Measurement of Power in International Relations." *International Organization* 30: 289-305.

Heider, F. 1946. "Attitudes and Cognitive Organizations." *Journal of Psychology* 21: 107-12.

Helpman, E., and P. R. Krugman. 1985. *Market Structure and Foreign Trade: Increasing Returns, Imperfect Competition, and the International Economy*. Cambridge, MA: MIT Press.

Heston, A., and R. Summers. 1991. "The Penn World Table (Mark 5): An Expanded Set of International Comparisons, 1950-1988." *Quarterly Journal of Economics* 106: 327-68.

———. 1994. *The Penn World Table (Mark 5.6)*.

Hirschman, A. O. 1945. *National Power and the Structure of Foreign Trade*. Berkeley and Los Angeles: University of California Press.

———. 1977. *The Passions and the Interests: Political Arguments for Capitalism before Its Triumph*. Princeton, NJ: Princeton University Press.

Hoffmann, S. 1965. *The State of War: Essays on the Theory and Practice of International Politics*. New York: Frederick A. Praeger.

Huber, J. H. 1996. *Rationalizing Parliament: Legislative Institutions and Party Politics in France*. Cambridge: Cambridge University Press.

Hufbauer, G., J. Schott, and K. Elliott. 1990a. *Economic Sanctions Reconsidered: History and Current Policy*. Washington, DC: Institute for International Economics.

————. 1990b. *Economic Sanctions Reconsidered: Supplemental Case Histories*. Washington, DC: Institute for International Economics.

Jones, D. M., S. A. Bremer, and J. D. Singer. 1996. "Militarized Interstate Disputes, 1816-1992: Rationale, Coding Rules, and Empirical Patterns." *Conflict Management and Peace Science* 15: 163-213.

Kadera, K. 1995. *Power Growth and Decay and Conflict Behavior in Dyadic Rivalries: A Dynamic Model*. Ph.D. Dissertation, Political Science. Urbana: University of Illinois at Urbana-Champaign.

Kant, I. 1991. *Kant's Political Writings [1795]*. Cambridge: Cambridge University Press.

Keohane, R., and H. Milner. 1996. "Internationalization and Domestic Politics: An Introduction." In *Internationalization and Domestic Politics*, edited by R. Keohane and H. Milner, 3-24. Cambridge: Cambridge University Press.

Keohane, R., and J. Nye. 1989. *Power and Interdependence*. Glenview, IL: Scott, Foresman.

Kim, S. Y. 1995. *Bilateral Conflict and Trade, 1948-86: The Role of Economic Interdependence in Conflict Processes*. Chicago: American Political Science Association.

King, G. 1989. *Unifying Political Methodology: The Likelihood Theory of Statistical Inference*. Cambridge: Cambridge University Press.

King, G., R. Keohane, and S. Verba. 1994. *Designing Social Inquiry*. Princeton, NJ: Princeton University Press.

Krugman, P., and M. Obstfeld. 1991. *International Economics: Theory & Policy*. New York: Harper Collins.

Landsburg, S. 1995. *Price Theory and Applications*. Minneapolis/St. Paul: West Publishing.

Lee, S. C., R. Muncaster, and D. Zinnes. 1994. "'The Friend of My Enemy is My Enemy': Modeling Triadic Internation Relationships." *Synthese* 100: 333-58.

Liao, T. 1994. *Interpreting Probability Models: Logit, Probit, and Other Generalized Linear Models*. Thousand Oaks, CA: Sage.

Long, J. S. 1997. *Regression Models for Categorical and Limited Dependent Variables*. Thousand Oaks, CA: Sage.

Mahnken, T. 1996. "Put the Cat Back in the Bag." *Far Eastern Economic Review,* April 18: 30.

Mansfield, E. 1994. *Power, Trade, and War.* Princeton, NJ: Princeton University Press.

Mansfield, E., and B. Pollins. 2001. "The Study of Interdependence and Conflict: Recent Advances, Open Questions, and Directions for Future Research." *Journal of Conflict Resolution* 45 (6):834-859.

————. 2003. *Economic Interdependence and International Conflict: New Perspectives on an Enduring Debate.* Ann Arbor: University of Michigan Press.

Marquez, J. 1990. "Bilateral Trade Elasticities." *Review of Economics and Statistics* 72: 70-77.

Martin, L. 1992. "Institutions and Cooperation: Sanctions during the Falkland Islands Conflict." *International Security* 16: 143-78.

McMillan, S. 1997. "Interdependence and Conflict." *Mershon International Studies Review* 41: 33-58.

Morrow, J. 1994. *Game Theory for Political Scientists.* Princeton, NJ: Princeton University Press.

————. 1999. "How Could Trade Affect Conflict?" *Journal of Peace Research* 36 (4):481-489.

————. 2003. "Assessing the Role of Trade as a Source of Costly Signals." in *Economic Interdependence and International Conflict: New Perspectives on an Enduring Debate.* Ann Arbor: University of Michigan Press.

North, D. 1990. *Institutions, Institutional Change and Economic Performance.* Cambridge: Cambridge University Press.

Oneal, J., F. Oneal, Z. Maoz, and B. Russett. 1996. "The Liberal Peace: Interdependence, Democracy, and International Conflict, 1950-85." *Journal of Peace Research* 33: 11-28.

Oneal, J. and B. Russett 1997. "The Classic Liberals Were Right: Democracy, Interdependence, and Conflict, 1950-1985." *International Studies Quarterly* 41: 267-94.

Papayoanou, P. 1996. "Interdependence, Institutions, and the Balance of Power." *International Security* 20: 42-76.

Polachek, S. 1978. "Dyadic Dispute: An Economic Perspective." *Peace Science Society (International) Papers* 28: 67-80.

————. 1980. "Conflict and Trade." *Journal of Conflict Resolution* 24: 55-78.

————. 1992. "Conflict and Trade: An Economics Approach to Political International Interactions." In *Economics of Arms Reduction and the Peace Process: Contributions from Peace Economics and Peace Science*, edited by W. Isard and C. Anderton. Amsterdam: North-Holland Press.

————. 1997. "Why Democracies Cooperate More and Fight Less: The Relationship Between International Trade and Cooperation." *Review of International Economics* 5: 295-309.

Polachek, S., Y.-C. Chang, and J. Robst. 1999. "Liberalism and Interdependence." *Journal of Peace Research* 36: 405-22.

Polachek, S., and J. McDonald. 1992. "Strategic Trade and the Incentive for Cooperation." In *Disarmament, Economic Conversions, and Management of Peace*, edited by M. Chatterji and L. R. Forcey, 273-84. New York: Praeger.

Richardson, L. F. 1960. *Statistics of Deadly Quarrels*. Pittsburgh: Boxwood Press and Chicago: Quadrangle Books.

Rosecrance, R. 1986. *The Rise of the Trading State*. New York: Basic Books.

Rosen, S. 1972. "War Power and the Willingness to Suffer." In *Peace, War, and Numbers*, edited by B. M. Russett, 167-83. Beverly Hills: Sage Publications.

Russett, B., and J. Oneal. 2001. *Triangulating Peace: Democracy, Interdependence, and International Organizations*. New York: W.W. Norton.

Sanger, D. 1996. "Analysis: Boeing, a Giant in Jets and Foreign Policy." *The New York Times*, December 17, 1996.

Singer, J. D., S. Bremer, and J. Stuckey. 1972. "Capability Distribution, Uncertainty, and Major Power War, 1820-1965." In *Peace, War, and Numbers*, edited by B. Russett, 19-48. Beverly Hills: Sage Publications.

Singer, J. D., and M. Small. 1972. *The Wages of War, 1816-1965*. New York: John Wiley.

Skaperdas, S., and C. Syropoulos. 1996. "Competitive Trade with Conflict." In *The Political Economy of Conflict and Appropriations*, edited by M. Garfinkel and S. Skaperdas, 73-96. Cambridge: Cambridge University Press.

Smith, A. 1996. "Diversionary Foreign Policy in Democratic Systems." *International Studies Quarterly* 40: 133-53.

Smith, C., and D. Hamilton. 1995. "Price of Entry Into China Rises Sharply: U.S. Firms Face Growing Pressure to Transfer Technology." *Wall Street Journal*, December 19, 1995: A14-A15.

Snyder, G., and P. Diesing. 1977. *Conflict Among Nations: Bargaining, Decision Making, and System Structure in International Crises*. Princeton, NJ: Princeton University Press.

Study Commission on U.S. Policy Toward Southern Africa. 1981. *South Africa: Time Running Out. The Report of the Study Commission on U.S. Policy Toward Southern Africa*. Berkeley: University of California Press, Foreign Policy Study Foundation.

U.S. Geological Survey 1973-1996. *Mineral Commodity Summaries, Mineral Industry and Mineral Commodity Profile*. Washington, DC: U.S. Geological Survey.

Vasquez, J. A. 1993. *The War Puzzle*. Cambridge: Cambridge University Press.

Wagner, H. 1988. "Economic Interdependence, Bargaining Power, and Political Influence." *International Organization* 42: 461-83.

Waltz, K. 1970. "The Myth of National Interdependence." In *The Multinational Corporation*, edited by C. P. Kindleberger. Cambridge, MA: MIT Press.

————. 1979. *Theory of International Politics*. New York: Random House.

Williamson, O. 1975. *Markets and Hierarchies: Analysis and Antitrust Implications*. New York: Free Press.

————. 1985. *The Economic Institutions of Capitalism: Firms, Markets, Relational Contracting*. New York: Free Press.

————. 1996. *The Mechanisms of Governance*. New York: Oxford University Press.

Wright, Q. 1965. *A Study of War*. Chicago: University of Chicago Press.

Index

About the Author

Mark J. C. Crescenzi, Assistant Professor of Political Science, earned his B.A. from the University of California at Irvine (1993) and both his M.A. and Ph.D. from the University of Illinois at Urbana-Champaign (2000). He teaches courses in international relations, including international conflict and national security. His current research employs formal and quantitative methods to focus on the link between international economic interdependence and conflict, the role of democracy and history in international conflict, and effects of democracy in the international system on conflict and state survival. He has recently contributed articles to the *American Journal of Political Science*, *The Journal of Politics*, *Conflict Management and Peace Science*, and *International Studies Quarterly*.